WHAT DOES IT MEAN TO "DO THIS"?

The Pro Ecclesia Series

Books in The Pro Ecclesia Series are "for the Church." The series is spon-sored by the Center for Catholic and Evangelical Theology, founded by Carl Braaten and Robert Jenson in 1991. The series seeks to nourish the Church's faithfulness to the gospel of Jesus Christ through a theology that is self-critically committed to the biblical, dogmatic, liturgical, and ethi-cal traditions that form the foundation for a fruitful ecumenical theology. The series reflects a commitment to the classical tradition of the Church as providing the resources critically needed by the various churches as they face modern and post-modern challenges. The series will include books by individuals as well as collections of essays by individuals and groups. The Editorial Board will be drawn from various Christian traditions.

OTHER TITLES IN THE SERIES INCLUDE:

- *The Morally Divided Body: Ethical Disagreement and the Disunity of the Church*, edited by Michael Root and James J. Buckley
- *Christian Theology and Islam*, edited by Michael Root and James J. Buckley
- *Who Do You Say That I Am?: Proclaiming and Following Jesus Today*, edited by Michael Root and James J. Buckley

What Does It Mean to "Do This"?

Supper, Mass, Eucharist

edited by

Michael Root &
James J. Buckley

CASCADE *Books* · Eugene, Oregon

WHAT DOES IT MEAN TO "DO THIS"?
Supper, Mass, Eucharist

Pro Ecclesia Series 4

Cascade Books
An Imprint of Wipf and Stock Publishers
199 W. 8th Ave., Suite 3
Eugene, OR 97401

www.wipfandstock.com

ISBN 13: 978-1-4982-2216-7

Cataloging-in-Publication data:

What does it mean to "do this"? : supper, mass, Eucharist / edited by Michael Root and James J. Buckley.

x + 144 pp. ; cm. —Includes bibliographical references.

Pro Ecclesia Series 4

ISBN 13: 978-1-4982-2216-7

1. Lord's Supper. 2. Lord's Supper—History of doctrines. I. Root, Michael, 1951–. II. Buckley, James Joseph, 1947–. III. Title. IV. Series.

BV825.3 .W48 2014

Manufactured in the U.S.A.

Contents

Contributors

Peter Bouteneff is Associate Professor of Systematic Theology at St. Vladimir's Orthodox Theological Seminary. He is author of *Sweeter than Honey: Orthodox Thinking on Dogma and Truth* (2006) and *Beginnings: Ancient Christian Readings of the Biblical Creation Narratives* (2008). From 1995 to 2000 he was Executive Secretary of Faith and Order at the World Council of Churches.

James J. Buckley is Professor of Theology at Loyola University Maryland. He is a member of the North American Lutheran Catholic dialogue and an associate director of the Center for Catholic and Evangelical Theology. He contributed to and edited *The Blackwell Companion to Catholicism* (2007).

George Hunsinger is the McCord Professor of Systematic Theology at Princeton Theological Seminary. He serves as a delegate to the official Reformed/Roman Catholic International Dialogue (2011–2017). Long known for his work on Karl Barth, he was the 2010 recipient of the Karl Barth Prize, awarded by the Union of Evangelical Churches in Germany. Among his recent books is *The Eucharist and Ecumenism: Let Us Keep the Feast* (2008).

Bruce D. Marshall is Lehman Professor of Christian Doctrine at the Perkins School of Theology, Southern Methodist University. He is the author of *Trinity and Truth* (2000), *Christology in Conflict: The Identity of a Saviour in Rahner and Barth* (1987), and several papers on Trinity, Christology, sacramental theology, and the theology of Thomas Aquinas. He is a member, and past President, of the Academy of Catholic Theology.

Martha Moore-Keish is Associate Professor of Theology at Columbia Theological Seminary in Decatur, Georgia. Her publications include *Do*

This in Remembrance of Me: A Ritual Approach to Reformed Eucharistic Theology (2008) and *Christian Prayer for Today* (2009). She currently serves as Reformed co-chair for the ecumenical dialogue between the World Communion of Reformed Churches and the Vatican's Pontifical Council for Promoting Christian Unity.

Francesca Aran Murphy is Professor of Systematic Theology at the University of Notre Dame du Lac. She was formerly Professor of Christian Philosophy in the University of Aberdeen, Scotland, where she taught from 1995 to 2010. Her major interests are theological aesthetics and ecclesiology. She is the author of *Christ, the Form of Beauty* (1995), *The Comedy of Revelation* (2000), *Art and Intellect in the Philosophy of Étienne Gilson* (2004), and *God Is Not a Story: Realism Revisited* (2007). She has also edited several volumes, including *The Providence of God: Deus Habet Consilium* (2009). Professor Murphy has translated three books. She is currently editing a book series with Bloomsbury Academic titled Illuminating Modernity.

Michael Root is Professor of Systematic Theology at The Catholic University of America and Executive Director of the Center for Catholic and Evangelical Theology. He was formerly the Director of the Institute for Ecumenical Research, Strasbourg, France.

Frank C. Senn, STS, is a retired pastor of the Evangelical Lutheran Church in America and Senior of the Society of the Holy Trinity. He is past president of the North American Academy of Liturgy and The National Liturgical Conference. He is author or editor of ten books, including *Christian Liturgy: Catholic and Evangelical* (1997), *A Stewardship of the Mysteries* (1999), *New Creation: A Liturgical Worldview* (2000), *The People's Work: A Social History of the Liturgy* (2006), and *An Introduction to Christian Liturgy* (2012). He has been a visiting professor at several seminaries and universities, including Garrett-Evangelical Theological Seminary and Nashotah House.

Telford Work is Professor of Theology at Westmont College and Chairman of its Religious Studies department. He is the author of *The Brazos Theological Commentary on the Bible: Deuteronomy* (2009), *Ain't Too Proud to Beg: Living through the Lord's Prayer* (2007), and *Living and Active: Scripture in the Economy of Salvation* (2002), and a contributor and signatory of *In One Body through the Cross: The Princeton Proposal for Christian Unity* (2003).

Preface

Michael Root and James J. Buckley

JESUS' MOST WELL-KNOWN MANDATE—after perhaps the mandate to love God and neighbor—was given at the Last Supper just before his death: "Do this in memory of me." Indeed, a case can be made that to "do this" is the source and summit of the way Christians carry out Jesus' love-mandate. Of course, Christians have debated what it means to "do this," and these debates have all too often led to divisions within and between them. These divisions seem to fly in the face of Jesus' mandate, causing some to wonder whether this is "really" the Lord's Supper we celebrate (compare 1 Corinthians 11). All turns on just what it means to "do this." The purpose of the Center for Catholic and Evangelical Theology's 2012 conference was to address at least some of the many aspects of this question—to address them together, as Catholics, Protestants, and Orthodox.

The Lutheran liturgical theologian and pastor Frank Senn provides a helpful overview of the history of Eucharist practice throughout the ages. George Hunsinger critically analyzes the Reformed theologian Karl Barth on three crucial topics in Eucharistic theology: the relations of Word and Sacrament, Real Presence, and Sacrifice. Bruce Marshall articulates a Catholic theology of presence through transubstantiation by focusing on "this is my body" as an identity statement. Peter Bouteneff not only surveys the positions of different Christian churches on whether Christians can receive communion at each other's Eucharists but also provides theological reasons for the distinctly Orthodox (and largely Roman Catholic) position on why Christians are not yet ready for (to use the odd term Bouteneff does not, thankfully, use) "intercommunion." Martha Moore-Keish, on another hand, makes a biblical and distinctively Reformed case for a more open Eucharistic table. Francesca Aran Murphy provides a profound Catholic theology of Eucharistic communion as sacrifice, while Telford Work brings in a Pentecostal perspective that challenges Orthodox and Catholic, Lutheran and Reformed alike. Discussions at the conference on the ordination of women were embedded in these other controversies.

There are surely other ways of ordering the essays: perhaps the first should be last and the last or the middle first. Readers can, of course, read one or other essay. But this book invites readers to compare the seven, seeking similarities and differences that relate to while transcending traditional disputes. Can Hunsinger's crucial exposition of Barth on the Eucharist or Murphy on Eucharistic sacrifice find a way between Bouteneff and Moore-Keish (and Senn) on communion? Can Marshall's explication of transubstantiation as arising from taking seriously "this is my body" as a simple identity statement, rather than a technical or philosophical term, move Catholics and Hunsinger's Barth closer to one another? Or does Work's Pentecostal practice call other Christians to a new way of hearing our different languages as voices of the same Spirit of communion? "The Eucharist," George Lindbeck once wrote, "tastes bitter in the divided church."[1] But we hope these essays do not promote the bitterness, except as a recognition of our Eucharistic sins. A truly Catholic and Evangelical theology and practice of the Supper can only arise from a careful listening and speaking with one another. We hunger together to "do this"—theologians and pastors and more ordinary folks.

---

1. "The Eucharist Tastes Bitter in the Divided Church," *Spectrum* (Yale Divinity School) 19 (1999) 1, 4–5.

1

Do This:
Eucharist and the Assembly's Liturgy

Frank C. Senn

WHAT DOES IT MEAN to "do this"? Before it means anything else, it means that we are to do what has been commanded. Many meanings cluster around the Eucharist, the Lord's Supper, the Mass, also known as Holy Communion and the Sacrament of the Altar, and these meanings are associated with the benefits offered. But there would be no benefits to receive if we didn't "do this" in the first place.

Touto poieite—"Do this." This is the command attached to the institution narrative cited by St. Paul as a tradition (*paradosis*). It is what he has received from the Lord and "handed over" to his congregation in Corinth. The command accompanies the words of Jesus over both the bread and the cup (1 Cor 11:24, 25).

The command to "do this" also appears in the institution narrative in St. Luke's Gospel (22:19). There is the textual problem of the two cups in the Lucan passion narrative (short text versus long text). No matter how one resolves the issue of one cup versus two cups, Luke certainly witnesses to the fact that Jewish meals did begin with a blessing over the cup as well as over the bread. The command to "do this in remembrance of me" after the words over the bread may also include the thanksgiving over the initial cup, even though the words identifying the poured out cup as "the new covenant in my blood" are connected to the second cup "after the supper" (*meta to deipnesai*) in the long text. In the *Didache*, chapters 9–10, there is an order similar to Luke's: blessing of the cup, blessing of the broken loaf, and thanksgiving at the end of the meal over the final cup.[1] The command to "do this" does not appear in the Matthean or Markan Gospels.

1. The Text

Exegetes and theologians have focused primarily on why we are to "do this." It is, as Paul's text says, "for my *anamnesis*." The whole idea of the eucharistic memorial is pretty central to the concerns of liturgical and sacramental theology, and a theology of eucharistic memorial has developed in relation to the eucharistic sacrifice.[2] But for the purpose of this presentation I will give *anamnesis* a simpler understanding.

When we come together as the church—the *ekklesia*, the assembly called out of the world—we are to celebrate the meal that Jesus instituted. In fact, the meetings of the early church were primarily for meals, as was the case with other associations in the Greco-Roman world.[3] Part of the meaning of the *anamnesis*, therefore, is simply to "do" the supper Jesus had with his disciples on the "night in which he was handed over"—not in the mimetic sense of dramatic reenactment, but in the expectation of Jesus' promise to be present in and to the celebration, specifically in the signs of bread and wine. "This is my body." "This is me."

The translation of the phrase "on the night he was handed over" is a bit problematic. In the Gospel narratives the word *paradidonai* can be correctly translated "betrayed" because in the story of the upper room Judas is intent on betraying Jesus, and Jesus tells him to get on with his sordid business. But Judas is not mentioned in the text received and quoted by Paul. Moreover, in Romans 8:32 Paul presents his view that God "handed over" (*paradidonai*) Jesus to death for all of us. So the term used in 1 Corinthians 11:23 could be understood by Paul to mean "the night in which *God* handed over Jesus." Within the Jewish reckoning of time, since the day

1. See Arthur Vööbus, *Liturgical Traditions in the Didache* (Stockholm: ETSE, 1968); Arthur Vööbus, *The Prelude to the Lukan Passion Narative* (Stockholm: ETSE, 1968).

2. See Kenneth Stevenson, *Eucharist and Offering* (New York: Pueblo, 1986).

3. See Philip A. Harland, *Associations, Synagogues, and Congregations: Claiming a Place in Ancient Mediterranean Society* (Minneapolis: Fortress, 2003).

begins the evening before, the Last Supper of Jesus with his disciples did take place on the day he died. Paul sees the death of Jesus, not his betrayal, proclaimed in the supper, by God's intention.

Moreover, the words of Jesus are all present tense, not past tense. Paul's text is not evoking a historical remembrance but a present reality—the presence of the crucified Lord who will come again as judge in the proclamation that occurs not just by words but by doing the supper. The judgment of the coming Lord is actually a present reality that is being experienced in the Corinthian community that has violated the ritual conditions in which the meal is to be celebrated by fracturing the body of the church at the table. "That is why many of you are weak and ill, and some have died," wrote Paul (1 Cor 11:30).

So what is it that we are supposed to do to obey this command of Jesus? It was Gregory Dix's thesis that the institution narrative provides a set of rubrics that implies a liturgical order.[4] Dix's further thesis was that the sevenfold actions spelled out in the institution narrative developed into the fourfold shape of the eucharistic liturgy when the sacramental meal was separated from the actual meal—resulting in Offertory, Consecration, Fraction, Administration. This thesis is generally regarded now as too facile. But just to rehearse the actions in the narrative related by Paul and probably followed in Corinth: they were to take a loaf of bread, give thanks over it, break it, and distribute it. Then, "after supper" (I'll explain this in a moment), they were to take the cup, give thanks over it, and drink from it. Furthermore, this is to be done in such a way that it demonstrates the oneness of the assembly at the table, not schism.

All of this seems straightforward enough. But we've been doing this supper for some two thousand years now, and over this span of time a lot of rubrical violations have occurred in various assemblies. Some haven't taken a loaf of bread; they've settled for the convenience of individual wafers. Some haven't offered up thanksgiving; they've recited the rubrics. Some have even fought over the breaking of bread (which, were a real loaf used, would need to be broken for distribution anyway). Some have not passed around or drunk from a cup; they've used individual straws, spoons, glasses, or received no wine/blood of Christ at all. In fact, the cup has been withheld from communicants at one time or another in most of our traditions. And some have not eaten the bread and drunk from the cup discerning the unity of body, the church; they have excluded baptized members

---

4. Gregory Dix, *The Shape of the Liturgy* (London: Dacre, 1945) 48ff.

of the assembly from the meal for non-disciplinary reasons. The threat of judgment that Paul says hangs over this meal suggests that the eucharistic assembly had better get its liturgical act together. So let me go through the things we are mandated to do to see how we might do them, beginning with the social context in which the Christian assembly in Corinth celebrated the Lord's Supper.

2. The Social Context

The social context of the celebration of the Lord's Supper was a gathering of the church in the house of a member, or in an inn rented for the occasion as other supper clubs did in the Greco-Roman world, to have a banquet. The form of the banquet was most likely a symposium. A symposium was a meal (which sometimes degenerated into a drinking party) in which the guests engaged in philosophic discussion. There were a number of literary symposia from ancient Greece and Rome, of which the most famous is probably Plato's.

Scholars like Blake Layerle[5] and Dennis E. Smith,[6] who have studied the meal customs of the ancient Greco-Roman world, see the symposium as the form of the banquet that lies behind the Jewish Passover Seder as well as the Christian Eucharist. Typically a symposium begins with a thanksgiving to the god of the feast, the sharing of food and wine, entertainment of sorts in the form of a dance, a poem, a drama, or even a philosophic proposition, followed by discussion of what has been presented, accompanied by additional cups of wine (with copious drinking!). The long night of discussion ended in Plato's *Symposium* with only Socrates, Aristophanes, and Agathon left, drinking out of a large cup that they passed around, and Socrates' two companions not being able to follow his argument because they were drowsy. The symposium broke up at daybreak; Socrates saw his companions home and went to the baths.[7]

The canonical Gospels also present a symposium on the night Jesus was betrayed that left the disciples drowsy and not able to watch with Jesus

---

5. Blake Leyerle, "Meal Customs in the Greco-Roman World," in *Passover and Easter: Origin and History to Modern Times*, ed. Paul F. Bradshaw and Lawrence A. Hoffman, Two Liturgical Traditions 5 (Notre Dame: University of Notre Dame Press, 1999) 29–61.

6. Dennis E. Smith, *From Symposium to Eucharist: The Banquet in the Early Christian World* (Minneapolis: Fortress, 2003).

7. *The Portable Plato*, ed. Scott Buchanan (New York: Viking, 1948) 186–87.

in the Garden of Gethsemane while he prayed to the Father that the next cup would pass from him. The symposium structure can best be seen in John 13–17. In the context of a meal, which is mentioned but not described, Jesus performs the dramatic action of washing his disciples' feet. This serves as the basis for discussion of the new commandment Jesus lays on his disciples (now called "friends"), that they love one another as he has loved them. Because this is a "last supper," there is also much discussion about Jesus' impending departure from his disciples. The symposium ends with Jesus' high priestly prayer to his Father on behalf of his disciples.

The symposium structure can also be seen in the Jewish Passover Seder in which, after the *berakoth* or blessings that mark the beginning of the meal, discussion ensues in connection with the strange food being eaten that night. Multiple cups of wine accompany the meal and discussion. The Seder ends with a prayer of thanksgiving for the meal (*birkat ha-mazon*).

There is no reason not to think that the Lord's Supper in the Corinthian church also followed the format of a meal (*deipnon*) with a symposium (*symposion*). The cup with its thanksgiving in Paul's text is "after supper." Is it possible that the words of Jesus over the cup cited by Paul—"Do this, as often as you drink it, in remembrance of me"—refer to the multiple cups of the symposium, and not to the frequency of the gatherings to share the meal since a comparable specification "as often as you *eat* this" does not accompany the command "do this" in connection with the bread? In other words, this banquet as a whole is the Lord's Supper, and the Lord himself is received—body and blood—throughout the meal in the bread that is broken and the multiple cups that are shared. References in 1 Corinthians 11:21 to some becoming drunk (as the guests were in Plato's *Symposium*) suggest that this was a real possibility. Hence, restraint is called for, not only in waiting for the slaves to arrive before the patrons and clients begin to eat, but also in the amount of wine consumed. There were obviously a lot of problems with the celebration of the Lord's Supper at Corinth. This advises us against taking the early church as a model for our liturgical practices today.

Whether the social problems connected with the celebration of the Lord's Supper at Corinth—patrons, clients, and slaves all sharing the same meal and the same menu[8]—contributed to separating the sacramental meal from the context of an actual meal, we cannot say. More likely, the

---

8. Gerd Theissen, *The Social Setting of Pauline Christianity*, ed. and trans. John H. Schütz (Philadelphia: Fortress, 1982) 145–74.

imperial ban on supper clubs imposed by Emperor Trajan early in the second century sealed this separation. We have the letter of Pliny the Younger, governor of Bithynia, to Emperor Trajan (ca. 112), in which he reports on his interrogation of Christians that they were complying with the edict forbidding secret societies.[9] Christian gatherings for an evening meal, especially in public places, could easily look to the Roman authorities like other assembles of clubs and societies; so the Christians ceased having the suppers. While we should resist the temptation to read one local witness as applying universally, since the Eucharist in the *Didache* is clearly in a meal context (and is not just an *agape* as some have suggested),[10] it is the case that the Eucharist increasingly became a morning celebration rather than an evening one and was celebrated using bread and wine alone. The Letter of Pliny indicates that Christians had already been assembling in the morning for a form of morning praise. He reports, "They gathered at daybreak to sing a hymn to Christ as to a god." Once the ban on supper clubs was relaxed or rescinded, Christians again gathered in the evening for a meal. But the restored evening meal became the *agape* or love feast, as we see in the *Apostolic Tradition,* which, in the Ethiopic text, began with a *lucernarium* (lamplighting).[11] But the Eucharist continued to be celebrated primarily in the morning.[12]

3. On What Day Is the Meal Done?

There is no reference in 1 Corinthians to *what day* the Lord's Supper was celebrated. Acts 2:46 says that the early Christian community broke bread in their homes "day by day" while they also attended the temple, which implies a daily Eucharist. Acts 20:7 says, "On the first day of the week, when we met to break bread." This could imply simply that this particular breaking of bread happened to occur on the first day of the week rather than that the congregation at Troas met to break bread *because* it was the first day of

9. Letter of Pliny to Emperor Trajan, in *Documents of the Christian Church,* ed. Henry Bettenson (New York: Oxford University Press, 1947) 6–7.

10. Thus J.-P. Audet, *Le Didachè. Instructions des apôtres* (Paris: Cerf, 1958).

11. Paul F. Bradshaw, Maxwell E. Johnson, and L. Edward Phillips, *The Apostolic Tradition: A Commentary,* ed. Harold W. Attridge (Minneapolis: Augsburg Fortress, 2002) 156–60.

12. See Willy Rordorf, *Sunday,* trans. A. A. K. Graham (Philadelphia: Westminster, 1968) 251–62.

the week. On the other hand, we note that John the Seer received his visions on the Lord's Day (Rev 1:10) and the visions of heavenly worship with all the Halleluia choruses included the marriage supper of the Lamb (19:1–9).

It is the case that the Eucharist came to be associated especially with the Lord's Day, even though its celebration on other days is not precluded. We have no reference to Christian worship on the Lord's Day that does not include the Eucharist, until the sixteenth-century Reformation. The issue for the Protestant reformers was not that the Lord's Supper or Holy Communion should not be celebrated on the Lord's Day but that it should not be celebrated without communicants. I will deal with the issue of communicants further on. But here I note that the emergence of the use of Ante-Communion in the Lutheran, Reformed, and Anglican traditions testifies to the views of Luther, Bucer, Calvin, and Cranmer that Holy Communion is the complete service; the service of the Word strains toward completion with the Meal.

The Lord's Day and the Lord's Supper are correlative: both celebrate the resurrection of Christ on the first day of the week, the day after the Sabbath. The fixed day of Christian worship became the day beyond the Sabbath, the day some of the church fathers called "the eighth day."[13] The "eighth day" refers to the eschatological character of the Lord's Day. But that eschatological character is connected with the presence of the risen and ascended Lord Christ who comes again as judge in the Eucharist. This Lord's Supper is the principal form of worship on the Lord's Day.

The post-resurrection meals of the disciples with the risen Christ are more paradigmatic for the church's Eucharist than the Last Supper. At the Last Supper everything was fraught with tension, and one of those at table with Jesus betrayed him. But the very presence of the risen Lord extending the hospitality of table fellowship to the same disciples who had failed him at the moment of the cross makes the meal itself a sign of forgiveness and reconciliation.

Here I would also note that days of fasting have not been considered appropriate for a eucharistic celebration, although Holy Communion might be administered from the pre-sanctified elements set aside from the Sunday Eucharist after the liturgy of the Word.[14] In the West the only use

13. See Jean Daniélou, *The Bible and the Liturgy* (Notre Dame: University of Notre Dame Press, 1956) 262–86.

14. See Robert Taft, *Beyond East and West: Problems in Liturgical Understanding* (Washington, DC: Pastoral, 1984) 66–68.

of the Mass of the Pre-sanctified has been on Good Friday. One does not feast and fast at the same time. Even the pre-sanctified must be received in the narrow window of opportunity between the end of one fast day and the beginning of another, usually just before Vespers which begins the next day. Those who would not receive communion from the pre-sanctified should not celebrate the eucharistic feast on fast days of the church year such as Ash Wednesday and Good Friday.

4. The Table of the Word

Returning to the feast: another aspect of the contribution of the symposium banquet to the form of the Christian eucharistic celebration is the joining of word and meal. Liturgical scholars have long pondered how a liturgy of the word that looks like the public synagogue liturgy with the reading and study of Scripture could have been joined with the meal liturgy that, in Judaism, would have been a more private domestic rite. The form of the symposium shows how a meal could have included readings and commentary, as was also the case with the Jewish Passover Seder. This unity of word and meal is not yet evident in the *Didache*, but it is evident in the Sunday liturgy described by Justin Martyr in his *Apology*, chapter 67, where he reports that "the memoirs of the apostles and the writings of the prophets are read as long as time permits. When the reader has finished, the president in a discourse urges and invites us to the imitation of these noble things."[15]

Later evidence shows that books of the Bible were read continuously. Many biblical commentaries by church fathers are actually homilies delivered on the biblical books. However, with the emergence of festival days (for example, Easter, the Ascension, Pentecost, Christmas) and seasons of devotion (Lent, Advent), specific readings having to do with the events commemorated in the life of Christ or the purpose of devotion (such as the catechumenate, repentance) were chosen. These are pericopes, or "cut out" selections. We see the development of a pericope system in Jerusalem in the fourth- and fifth-century pilgrimage rites. A pericope system attributed to Jerome, the *Comes Hieronymi* ("Jerome" = "Jerusalem"), became very influential in the Western Church through the Roman Gelasian and Gregorian Sacramentaries imported by Pippin and Charlemagne into the

---

15. "The First Apology of Justin, the Martyr," ed. and trans. Edward Rochie Hardy, in *Early Christian Fathers*, ed. Cyril C. Richardson, Library of Christian Classics 1 (Philadelphia: Westminster, 1953) 287.

Frankish Church, where it was augmented by Alcuin to include additional days observed in the Frankish Church and the whole season of Advent. Alcuin also eliminated Old Testament readings and shortened many of the epistle and gospel readings. This became the basis of the so-called historic one-year lectionary.

The Reformation was at first drawn to the ancient practice of continuous reading (*lectio continua*) of biblical books with preaching through those books. This became a reality in the Reformed churches. But in the Lutheran churches as well as in the Church of England, there was a preference for the historic lectionary with its pericope system. The Roman Rite after the Council of Trent also retained this historic lectionary, so that there were many similarities in the pericopes for the church year lectionary in the Roman Catholic, Lutheran, and Anglican churches. There actually was an ecumenical liturgical consensus in the West before the Second Vatican Council.

A concern was expressed by the bishops at the Second Vatican Council that the people should be exposed to a greater selection of Scripture, including the Old Testament. Certainly much of the Bible was read in the offices of the Liturgy of the Hours, but most people attended only masses or engaged in paraliturgical devotions. The Constitution on the Sacred Liturgy (*Sacrosanctam Concilium*) of the Second Vatican Council called for "more reading from holy Scripture in sacred celebrations, and it is to be more varied and suitable" (35.1) and also for preaching that "draws its content from scriptural and liturgical sources" (35.2). In fulfilling of this desire of the Council, the Concilium for the Implementation of the Constitution developed and published *Ordo Lectionum Missae* with the reformed Mass in 1969.

The Roman Lectionary for the Mass presented a new three-year series of readings for the Mass that supplanted the historic one-year lectionary in the Roman Catholic Church. It added an Old Testament reading with a responsorial psalm and even included a *lectio continua* principle in the epistle readings during ordinary time. In short order other churches adopted versions of the Roman three-year lectionary. Versions of the Roman three-year lectionary were included in the *Lutheran Book of Worship* (1978) and in *The Book of Common Prayer* of the Episcopal Church (1979). In adopting versions of this lectionary, Lutherans and Anglicans/Episcopalians in North America departed from their sister churches in Europe.

A number of churches were using versions of the Roman three-year lectionary, but there were discrepancies in the choice of readings, especially in the season after Pentecost. The North American–based Consultation on Common Texts (CCT) worked with the international English Language Liturgical Consultation (ELLC) to put together a revision of the Roman Catholic three-year lectionary, which appeared in 1983 as the Common Lectionary.[16] This Common Lectionary found a way to incorporate some of the variations in the three-year lectionaries as options and added the further option of a quasi *lectio continua* Old Testament track during the Time after Pentecost. (The provision of options means that it is not totally common in the sense of uniformity.) After a nine-year trial period, a Revised Common Lectionary was publicly released in 1992. It was immediately included in the worship books of the United Methodist and Presbyterian churches (1992 and 1993, respectively) and was subsequently adopted in whole or with emendation by eight other denominations in the United States, four denominations in Canada, as well as by the Anglican and Reformed churches in the United Kingdom and Australia. A petition to the Vatican to adopt the Revised Common Lectionary as the Lectionary for the Roman Mass was turned down.

We should note, however, as Fritz West has pointed out, that while Protestants and Roman Catholic use practically the same lectionary, they approach it with different hermeneutics.[17] The concern of the Protestant lectionaries to not skip verses and to provide the contextual lead-in verses in the pericopes indicates a primary concern for preaching the Word. The concern in the Roman Lectionary is to hear the living voice of Christ at the table; hence the scriptural or historical context is not so important. The Roman Lectionary is a eucharistic lectionary, not a preaching lectionary, even though it was, as the late Methodist liturgist James F. White said, Catholicism's greatest gift to Protestant biblical preaching. We should also note that the Revised Common Lectionary is not used as a eucharistic lectionary in Protestant churches because for most Protestant congregations most of their Sunday services are not the Eucharist.

16. See Horace T. Allen Jr., "*Common Lectionary*: Origins, Assumptions, Issues," *Studia Liturgica* 21 (1991) 14–30.

17. Fritz West, *Scripture and Memory: The Ecumenical Hermeneutic of the Three-Year Lectionary* (Collegeville, MN: Liturgical/Pueblo, 1997).

5. Bread and Wine

We turn next to what Augustine called the "visible words" of the sacrament: the bread and the wine. To talk about the Eucharist without saying anything about its elements is like talking about marriage without mentioning sex. The bread and wine are, in fact, the *sacramenta*, the sacred signs.

The Last Supper of Jesus, according to Synoptic Gospels, was a Passover Seder for which unleavened bread was required. However, the Eucharist in the early church was not a continuation of the Passover Seder. So unleavened bread is not required for the Eucharist. The fact that the Western Church increasingly used unleavened bread became a source of contention between the Greek and Latin churches. In the ninth century the use of unleavened bread had become universal and obligatory in the West, while the Greeks, desiring to emphasize the distinction between the Jewish *Pesach* and the Christian Pasch, continued the exclusive offering of leavened bread. The issue became divisive when the provinces of Byzantine Italy, which were under the authority of the Patriarch of Constantinople, were forcibly incorporated into the Church of Rome following their invasion by the Norman armies. The Byzantine Rite was suppressed in southern Italy and replaced with the Latin Rite and its use of unleavened wafers. Patriarch Michael Cærularius of Constantinople responded to this situation in 1053 by ordering all the Latin churches in the Byzantine capital to be closed, and the Latin monks to be expelled. In retaliation Greek churches were closed in Rome. This was obviously a political issue. But the theological touchstone became the use of unleavened wafers. In popular Greek opinion, the flour and water wafers of the "Franks" were not bread; their sacrifices were invalid; they were Jews not Christians. Their lifeless bread could only symbolize a soulless Christ; therefore, they had clearly fallen into the heresy of Apollinaris. The controversy became a key factor in producing the East-West Schism of 1054. Cærularius found the issue politically useful in his conflict with the Latins. This question of azyms brought forth a cloud of pamphlets, and made a deeper impression on the popular imagination than the abstruse controversy of the Filioque. But it caused little or no discussion among the theologians at the Councils of Lyons and Florence. At the latter Council the Greeks admitted agreement with the Latin contention that the consecration of the elements was equally valid with leavened and unleavened bread; it was decreed that the priests of either rite should conform to the custom of their respective church.

Two seemingly contradictory developments dominated eucharistic faith and practice in the Western Middle Ages. On the one hand the eucharistic debates of the ninth and eleventh centuries led to the formulation and promulgation of the dogma of transubstantiation. Yet in spite of the growing belief that the bread changes into body at the words of Christ, there remained an awareness that the Eucharist is essentially food intended for nourishment and great concern was shown for the bread and wine as food and drink. The wheaten bread and the fine grape wine satisfies hunger and quenches thirst. The whole moral allegory of *Piers Plowman* is constructed around images of ploughing and food production, a merging of images of physical food and spiritual food. So in spite of the eucharistic realism of the high scholastic period, the Augustianian distinction between the visible sign (*sacramentum*) and the sacramental reality behind it (*res*) continued to persist in pastoral teaching. In spite of a formulary such as Hugh of St. Cher's, that "when the bread becomes Christ's body, nothing at all remains of the bread, that is, nothing is shared in common,"[18] great care was taken in the production of the bread. Baking wafers became a ritualized procedure in religious houses, accompanied by the chanting of psalms. Ministers in parish churches who baked wafers were to be vested in their surplices. The wafers were to be baked in a vessel coated with wax rather than in fat or oil so that they were not burned.[19] A twelfth-century tract answered the question of why only wheat was used with the answer that it is because Christ compared himself to a grain of wheat that falls into the ground and dies.[20]

In liturgical renewal after the Second Vatican Council there has been a preference to use whole loaves of bread rather than individual wafers. More recently, however, we have become aware that some people have gluten allergies, and effort has been made to provide the option of gluten-free bread for Holy Communion, which has resulted in the production of gluten-free wafers. Pastoral discretion suggests finding discreet ways of accommodating this need.

Communion wine has drawn far less attention. The wine used in antiquity was strong. It was cut with water for social drinking. Nevertheless, it was more vulnerable to mishap in its handling than the wafers. By the twelfth century the cup was withheld from lay communicants. It was

18. Cited in Miri Rubin, *Corpus Christi: The Eucharist in Late Medieval Culture* (Cambridge: Cambridge University Press, 1991) 37.

19. Ibid., 42.

20. Ibid., 38.

replaced in many places by a sip of unconsecrated wine, for symbolic symmetry and to make it easier to swallow the host. Synodical legislation shows concern that the communion wine should be fresh, to avoid consecrating vinegar in the chalice, and that care should be taken that there should be more wine than water in the chalice.

The Protestant reformers restored the cup to lay communicants. Communion cups even increased in size to accommodate more drinking from them. But with the rise of the science of epidemiology, and the tuberculosis epidemics of the late nineteenth and early twentieth centuries, fear of contagion resulted in bans on the use of common drinking containers, including the communion cup. Individual glasses became the rule in most Protestant congregations. In 1869 Thomas Bramwell Welch, a strong supporter of the temperance movement, discovered a method of pasteurizing grape juice that halted the fermentation process. This enabled him to produce a nonalcoholic wine to be used for church services in his hometown of Vineland, New Jersey. In the wake of the temperance movement, grape juice was routinely substituted for wine in many Protestant congregations. This also increased the use of individual glasses since the beverage lacked the alcoholic content to kill bacteria. In spite of lack of scientific evidence that the common communion cup contributes to the spread of disease, people's fears of contagion have not easily been overcome. Outbreaks of new viruses have caused further bans on the use of communion cups, so that the restoration of the cup has often been accomplished only through the practice of intinction (in which people's far more germ-ridden finger tips get into the wine). Consistency would suggest that the restoration of a common drinking cup should be matched by the restoration of a single loaf and that the Lord's Supper should look more like a meal. Also the idea of a common meal suggests one menu with only a discreet minimum of options.

6. Great Thanksgiving

The central text of the liturgy of the meal is the eucharistic prayer, sometimes now called the Great Thanksgiving. The narratives of the institution of the Lord's Supper in the New Testament, especially Matthew 26:26–27 and Mark 14:22–23, indicate that Jesus took bread and "blessed it" (*eulogysas*) and after supper took a cup of wine and "gave thanks" (*eucharistysas*) over it. This conforms with the Jewish meal prayer tradition that we see in the *Berakoth* tractate in the Mishnah: the blessing of God for the bread before the meal and the thanksgiving over the cup at the end of the meal. This same division of prayers is seen in the *Didache* 9–10. The prayers before and after the meal would not be brought together into one unified eucharistic prayer or series of prayers until the actual meal fell away and thanksgiving was given over the bread and cup together. The earliest extant unified eucharistic prayers would be the third-century East Syrian Anaphora of Addai and Mari and the eucharistic prayer in the so-called *Apostolic Tradition* attributed to Hippolytus of Rome.

The history of the eucharistic prayer is very complicated but thoroughly studied.[21] The eucharistic prayers in the *Didache* include no institution narrative. It is probably lacking also in the East Syrian Anaphora of Addai and Mari. There is an institution narrative in the *Apostolic Tradition*, but this church order is reconstructed from versions that appear later than the third century and not in the Greek in which the *Apostolic Tradition* was most likely written. What is not debatable is that the Words of Institution have a place in fourth-century anaphoras.

It is now well established that there was no single apostolic Eucharist from which everything evolved. It is more likely that different models developed in various local churches and that there was a tendency for churches to borrow from one another and then, at a later point in history, to accentuate differences as the local churches came under the hegemony of patriarchal churches (Antioch, Alexandria, Rome, Constantinople, and Jerusalem).

Two elements divide the East and the West: the *epiclesis* and the oblation. An invocation (*epiclesis*) of the Holy Spirit developed in the Eastern churches; the Holy Spirit is called down on the bread and wine to manifest or change them into the body and the blood. The *epiclesis* is most highly developed in the West Syrian/Byzantine anaphoras of St. Basil and St. John Chrysostom. This is also the area in the church that was most engaged in the Christological and Trinitarian controversies of the fourth and fifth centuries. The West Syrian prayers developed a Trinitarian scheme that has been most attractive to those working on worship books in the late twentieth century. The scheme is as follows:

Praise of God for his work of creation leading to the Sanctus

21. For a synopsis of the current state of scholarship, see Paul F. Bradshaw, *The Search for the Origins of Christian Worship*, 2nd ed. (Oxford: Oxford University Press, 2002) 118–43.

Remembrance of the Son leading to the institution narrative

Offering of the gifts and invocation of the Holy Spirit leading to commemorations and intercessions

Concluding Trinitarian doxology

Bridge phrases connect the different parts of the prayer. After the Sanctus there is: "Holy are you and all holy . . ." leading to a recital of salvation history. After the Words of Institution there is a summary of the remembrance (the anamnesis): "Remembering therefore the cross, tomb, resurrection on the third day, ascension, enthronement in heaven, second and glorious coming . . ." leading to the offering—"we offer you your own from what is your own" (oblation)—leading to the *epiclesis*—"We implore you to send your Holy Spirit . . ." The progression of thought is: remembering, we offer, and we implore (*memores . . . offerimus . . . petimus*).

As theories of the eucharistic presence of Christ developed in the fourth century, it is not surprising that Eastern fathers (e.g., Theodore of Mopsuestia, John Chrysostom) pointed to the work of the Holy Spirit in bringing about the sacramental union of bread/body and wine/blood, whereas the Western fathers Ambrose and Augustine pointed to the efficacy of the words of Christ to make the sacrament.

There is an oblation or offering of the gifts in all the prayers because the eucharistic prayer said everything that needed to be said about the eucharistic rite, and separate offertory prayers are a later development. But the element of oblation became more highly developed in the Alexandrian and Roman prayers than in the Syrian, East or West. An early version of the Egyptian eucharistic tradition is the eucharistic prayer in the fourth-century Prayer Book (*Euchologion*) of Bishop Sarapion of Thmuis in lower Egypt. After an extensive Trinitarian and cosmic introduction leading to the Sanctus, there is immediately an offering of the bread—"the likeness of the holy body"—leading to the words of Christ about the bread. This is followed by a quote from the *Didache* prayer about the bread scattered over the mountains gathered together to become one loaf as the church is gathered together out of every nation and becomes one, leading to an offering of the cup—"the likeness of the blood"—and the words of Christ over the cup, followed by an invocation of the Word (*Logos*)—not the Holy Spirit!—on the bread and cup that they may become the body of the Word and the blood of Truth. In the Anaphora of St. Mark the introduction is expanded beyond all bounds and includes copious intercessions for the living and commemorations of the faithful departed and a petition to receive the thank-offerings of those who offered sacrifices. As in Sarapion, the Words of Institution are used as a warrant for the oblation. The element of oblation is the theological emphasis in the Alexandrian tradition.

Egypt was the breadbasket of Rome. There was a lot of commerce between Rome and Alexandria. We should remember this when we consider influences on the Roman Canon. We have no extant Roman eucharistic prayer before the Canon included in the *Codex Reginensis 316* (a Gelasian Saramentary) of the eighth century. There are only portions of a eucharistic prayer cited by Ambrose in *De Sacramentis* (*On the Sacraments*), but they are enough to show the influence of the Alexandrian eucharistic tradition.[22] It is not surprising, therefore, to find the elements of oblation, intercession, and commemoration so pervasive in the Roman Canon, and the Words of Institution, from the standpoint of literary and theological analysis, serving as the warrant for the oblation (taking the bread and cup) rather than the climax of a narration of salvation history, as in the West Syrian prayers.

The emphasis throughout the Canon is on "our gifts," which are offered for the church and for particular needs. Martin Luther believed that this was the reverse of the purpose of the sacrament, which was that the faithful receive the gift of communion in Christ.[23] The heart of the sacrament is not gifts we offer but gifts we receive. The fact that the most common form of the mass was the votive mass offered for special intentions for the living and the dead and paid for with mass stipends, caused Luther to see works righteousness and blasphemy in the heart of the mass itself.[24] People were being taught to offer their gifts in expectation of benefits that Christ has already secured in his once-for-all atoning sacrifice on the cross. The liturgical consequence of this critique of the mass, in Luther's view and action, was to delete all the prayers of the Canon after the Sanctus and retain only the Words of Institution—sung aloud using the gospel reciting chant as a proclamation of the gospel, as we see in his German Mass. Other reformers tried their hand at rewriting the eucharistic prayer in order to express more clearly the Reformation axis of justification by faith/atonement

22. See Ralph Keifer, "Oblation in the First Part of the Roman Canon: An Examination of a Primitive Eucharistic Structure and Theology in Early Italian and Egyptian Sources," PhD diss., University of Notre Dame, 1972.

23. See Carl F. Wisløff, *The Gift of Communion: Luther's Controversy with Rome on Eucharistic Sacrifice*, trans. Joseph M. Shaw (Minneapolis: Augsburg, 1964).

24. See Martin Luther, *The Babylonian Captivity of the Church*, in *Luther's Works* (Philadelphia: Fortress, 1959) 36:35–57.

by the all-sufficient sacrifice of Christ, perhaps most notably Thomas Cranmer, archbishop of Canterbury and primary author of *The Book of Common Prayer* (1549, 1552).[25]

Late twentieth-century worship books have moved away from having only one canon and provided multiple options of Great Thanksgivings.[26] The decision to provide four eucharistic prayers in the Roman Missal of 1969 was made by Pope Paul VI himself. Other churches followed this lead by providing multiple eucharistic prayers. Eucharistic renewal has privileged the West Syrian anaphora structure because of its Trinitarian structure and narrative elements. However, this has not been without its problems. Most of the new prayers have retained the Western tradition of a variable proper preface, which really limits the cosmological element in the introductory part of the prayer because the Western preface focuses on the specific work of Christ as celebrated in the seasons of the church year. The Roman Catholic prayers in particular have had difficulty with an *epiclesis* on the bread and wine *after* the Words of Institution, preferring such an episclesis before the institution narrative (even in Prayer IV, based on the Anaphora of St. Basil). Thus, with allowances for particular denominational emphases, a common pattern of eucharistic prayer has emerged that contains these parts:

> Preface with proper leading to
>
> the Sanctus
>
> Post-sanctus narrative of salvation history leading to the Words of Institution
>
> Memorial acclamation
>
> Anamnesis (Remembrance of the saving work of Christ)
>
> Epiclesis (invocation of the Holy Spirit with petition for the benefits of communion
>
> Intercession and commemoration.
>
> Concluding Trinitarian doxology

25. See Aidan Kavanagh, *The Concept of Eucharistic Memorial in the Canon Revisions of Thomas Cranmer, Archbishop of Canterbury, 1533–1556* (St. Meinrad, IN: Abbey, 1964).

26. See Frank C. Senn, ed., *New Eucharistic Prayers: An Ecumenical Study of Their Development and Structure* (Mahwah, NJ: Paulist, 1987).

A study of the eucharistic tradition offers other models of eucharistic prayer that might serve as inspiration for new ways of observing the command of Christ to give thanks over the bread and cup. But certainly a concern in new eucharistic prayers would be to express the fullness of eucharistic faith. As the Swedish bishop and theologian Yngve Brilioth demonstrated already in 1930, the Eucharist admits of multiple meanings and cannot be reduced to one or two. He highlighted thanksgiving, fellowship, memorial, and sacrifice, with the element of the mystery of the real presence of Christ pervading them all.[27] Geoffrey Wainwright has also recovered the early church's eschatological understanding of the Eucharist,[28] and eschatological elements such as the *Maranatha* acclamation ("Come, Lord Jesus") and the Memorial acclamation are found in current prayers. Those churches or local congregations that refuse the use of a full eucharistic prayer deprive their people of exposure to the fullness of eucharistic meaning. The eucharistic prayer also served as the fullest expression of Trinitarian doctrine before the creeds found a place in the liturgical order since these prayers were offered to Father, through the Son, in the Holy Spirit. It is lamentable that some churches or local congregations today garble the doctrine of the Trinity precisely in the Great Thanksgiving. Thanksgiving is offered to the Father (not just to "God") through the Son in the Holy Spirit.

7. Communion and Communicants

The communion rite begins with the breaking of bread. The bread needs to be broken for distribution, but St. Paul already saw a symbolic implication in the act: "The bread that we break, is it not a sharing [*koinonia*] in the body of Christ?" (1 Cor 10:16).

Gregory Dix's thesis that this action became the ceremonial fraction in the historic eucharistic liturgies is criticized today (along with his contention that the "taking" of bread and wine became the offertory). Nevertheless, the fraction played an important part in both the consecration and the extended sharing in the body of Christ. In the Roman *ordines* in the early Middle Ages (ca. 700–800) the bread was broken during the singing of the *Agnus Dei*. Bread from the altar was taken to other bishops who broke it into sacks containing the bread offerings of the people held by acolytes.

27. Yngve Brilioth, *Eucharistic Faith and Practice, Evangelical and Catholic*, trans. A. G. Hebert (London: SPCK,1965; originally published in Swedish in 1927).

28. Geoffrey Wainwright, *Eucharist and Eschatology* (London: Epworth, 1971).

This served as a kind of consecration by contagion for the communion of the people. A second piece of the consecrated bread was brought to the pope on a large paten; he broke off a piece and placed it in the chalice; the text of the prayer indicated that this commingling of bread and wine represented one Lord. The pope ate the bread and drank from the chalice. The chalice was then taken to the scyphus that contained the wine offerings of the people and wine from the chalice was poured into it to consecrated it for the communion of the people (who drank from a straw). The communion of the clergy and people then commenced.[29] Other pieces of bread were sent to other churches in the city where it was added to the elements in those Eucharists as a *fermentum* that demonstrated the unity of the whole local church in its bishop's Eucharist, a piece was reserved as *sancta* to be added to the next Eucharist, and some was reserved as *viaticum* for the communion of the sick and dying.

With the increased use of unleavened bread in the Latin rite and the manufacture of small wafers or hosts, the purpose of the fraction for the communion lost its significance, even though three pieces continued to be broken off the large priest's host and a piece was dropped into the cup for the commingling.[30] Pieces of the host were broken and arranged on the corporal. Allegorical significance was assigned to each arrangement in the commentaries on the Mass. The breaking of bread represented, in a symbolic way, the presence of Christ.

It is not surprising that, in the Reformation, Lutherans rejected the fraction while the Reformed gravitated to it.[31] In Electoral Brandenburg, where the Reformed House of Hohenzollern ruled over a Lutheran population, lay people, who might not understand the subtleties of sacramental theology, knew they were receiving a Lutheran or a Reformed pastor by whether he elevated the host or broke the bread.[32]

Contemporary debates in Anglican and Lutheran churches have been waged over whether words should be spoken in connection with the

---

29. Theodore Klauser, *A Short History of the Western Liturgy*, trans. John Halliburton (Oxford: Oxford University Press, 1969) 67–68.

30. See Joseph A. Jungmann, *The Mass of the Roman Rite: Its Origin and Development*, trans. Francis A. Brunner (Westminster, MD: Christian Classics, 1986) 2:303–21.

31. See Oliver K. Olson, "Contemporary Trends in Liturgy Viewed from the Perspective of Classical Lutheran Theology," *Lutheran Quarterly* 26 (1974) 125–34.

32. See Bodo Nischan, *Prince, People, and Confession: The Second Reformation in Brandenburg* (Philadelphia: University of Pennsylvania Press, 1994) 138–39.

breaking of the bread or let the action speak for itself.[33] A good compromise is the invitation, "Holy things for the holy people."

Who are the holy people? The baptized. In the sacramental economy Holy Communion is the completion of the process of Christian initiation. Those who are baptized should be communed at the same service as their baptism. The baptism of infants and young children did not, at first, seem to present an obstacle to this sequence, and this has remained the pattern in the Eastern churches. For reasons too complicated to rehearse here, in the Western Church baptism and first communion were separated for children.[34] Confession and/or confirmation eventually intervened between baptism and first communion. The Fourth Lateran Council in 1215 laid on all who had attained an age of discretion the obligation of making a confession to a priest before receiving communion. A voluntary form of private confession to the pastor was retained in early Lutheran practice and was usually, though not necessarily, connected with receiving Holy Communion. The sacrament of confirmation was haphazardly performed in the medieval church and sometimes preceded first communion and sometimes followed it. In the Reformed Church, in response to Anabaptist charges of lax spiritual discipline in the churches of the magisterial Reformation, catechetical instruction and the rite of confirmation construed as an affirmation of baptism became a prerequisite for first communion. Lutherans adopted this practice during the Age of Rationalism, beginning in the Kingdom of Prussia. Only in recent years has first communion been separated from confirmation and the age of first communion has steadily dropped in Protestant churches.

The new controversy today is whether unbaptized worshipers should be invited to receive Holy Communion because of hospitality associated with a meal. Some seekers begin to receive communion before they are baptized; reception of communion may even lead to their desire to be baptized. The move from table to font is becoming more widespread and has been hotly debated, especially in the Episcopal Church.[35] The fenced table

33. The proposed text, "Reveal yourself to us, O Lord, in the breaking of bread, as once you revealed yourself to the disciples," in The Holy Communion, *Contemporary Worship 2*, prepared by the Inter-Lutheran Commission on Worship in 1970, did not find its way into the text of The Holy Communion in *Lutheran Book of Worship* (1978).

34. See J. D. C. Fisher, *Christian Initiation: Baptism in the Medieval West* (London: SPCK, 1965) 101–8.

35. See J. Barrington Bates, "Giving What Is Sacred to Dogs? Welcoming All to the Eucharistic Feast," *Journal of Anglican Studies* 3 (2005) 53–74; James Farwell, "Baptism,

today seems inhospitable, exclusionary, and unchristian to many pastors and lay people. The invitation "Holy things for the holy people" would preclude the communion of those who have not been made holy by holy baptism. Lacking among those who promote an open table is an understanding that the whole sacramental economy participates in the paschal mystery. We are included in Christ's passover from death to life in holy baptism and Holy Communion. In the ancient church there would be no question about welcoming the unbaptized to the Lord's table. They wouldn't even be near the table. "Let all catechumens depart." The verses at the end of the table prayers in *Didache* 10:6 state, "If anyone is holy, let him come. If anyone is not, let him repent."[36] I would propose that holiness is not just a moral state, it is a ritual state. The holy people are those whom God has made his own in holy baptism. Repentance and baptism go together.

A further challenge to welcoming guests to the Lord's table is posed by Christian disunity and a mobile society. Should communion should be open to baptized Christians from other churches who come as visitors to a liturgy? This issue is bound up with ecclesiastical discipline—namely, being in fellowship with the bishop or the denomination. But the issue wouldn't even be considered if the sacramental economy were intact. We have separated baptism and communion rather than seeing them as part of a complete initiation into the paschal mystery of Jesus Christ. If our assembly recognizes someone's baptism, we must also recognize them as communicants and admit them to the Lord's table; it is their baptismal birthright. Conversely, if someone from another tradition presents himself or herself for Holy Communion, he or she should recognize that participation implies a tacit acceptance of the faith of this assembly.

Eucharist, and the Hospitality of Jesus: On the Practice of 'Open Communion,'" *Anglican Theological Review* 86 (2004) 215–38; Kathryn Tanner, "In Praise of Open Communion: A Rejoinder to James Farwell," *Anglican Theological Review* 86 (2004) 473–85; James Farwell, "A Brief Reflection on Kathryn Tanner's Response to 'Baptism, Eucharist, and the Hospitality of Jesus,'" *Anglican Theological Review* 87 (2005) 303–10; Stephen Edmondson, "Opening the Table: The Body of Christ and God's Prodigal Grace," *Anglican Theological Review* 91 (2009) 213–34.

36. Kurt Niederwimmer, *The Didache: A Commentary*, trans. Linda M. Maloney, ed. Harold Attridge (Minneapolis: Fortress, 1998) 155.

8. Preparation for Holy Communion

Let there be no mistake: the fundamental preparation for receiving Holy
Communion is baptism. Catechesis precedes baptism for adults and follows baptism for young children. Even so, in the ancient church the mysta-
gogic catecheses was given only after the newly baptized had experienced
the sacraments. In the case of the baptism and communion of infants, instruction in the meaning of Holy Communion can be given after receiving
communion just as instruction in the meaning of baptism is given after the
fact. Formation and nurture within the family is provided as one takes one's
place at the family table.

There can also be disagreements within the family that cause separation at the table. The angry family member gets up and leaves—or, in the
case of a naughty child, is told to leave. So schism happens not only between
Christian communities but also within them for reasons of scandal and sin.
When this happens reconciliation must occur. This is undoubtedly what is
intended by the instruction in chapter 14 of the *Didache*: "Assembling on every Sunday of the Lord's Day, break bread and give thanks, confessing your
faults beforehand, so that your sacrifice may be pure. Let no one engaged
in a dispute with his comrade join you until they have been reconciled, lest
your sacrifice be profaned."[37] "Confessing your sins" does not here refer
to something like a Brief Order for Confession and Forgiveness or even
to private confession, which are medieval developments, but to an act of
reconciliation. Later church orders like the *Apostolic Constitutions* said that
bishops should hear cases on Mondays. This would allow the greatest possible time for disputes to be resolved and for reconciliation to be effected
before the Sunday Eucharist. Reconciliation is what "the peace of the Lord"
is all about, which, in the Roman rite occurs just before communion, but in
other rites occurs before the offering of gifts. Martin Luther regarded "the
peace of the Lord" as "a public absolution of the sins of the communicants,
the true voice of the gospel announcing remission of sin, and therefore the
one and most worthy preparation for the Lord's Table, if faith holds to these
words as coming from the mouth of Christ himself."[38] The purpose of the
sacrament, as Luther expressed it in the post-communion prayer in his

37. Ibid., 194.

38. "An Order of Mass and Communion for the Church at Wittenberg," 1523, in *Luther's Works* (Philadelphia: Fortress, 1965) 53:28–29.

German Mass, is "to strengthen us . . . in faith toward thee, and in fervent love among us all."[39]

We have pastorally encouraged forms of personal preparation such as fasting. In his *Small Catechism* Luther said that "he is truly worthy and well prepared who believes these words: 'for you' and 'for the forgiveness of sins.'" He added that "the words 'for you' require truly believing hearts."[40] But the assembly must also prepare itself to worthily celebrate the Eucharist, Lord's Supper, Mass. Here the words of St. Paul apply: we must eat the bread and drink from the cup in such a way that we "discern the body" (1 Cor 11:28–29). The body to be discerned is the church assembled in peace and unity at the Lord's table.

When we return to the symposium form of the Lord's Supper, which provided the context for the assembly's meeting, we can imagine that the apostle's letter was read to the assembly during the dinner. If so, he was criticizing the assembly's Eucharist in the very context in which they were doing it. The assembly's liturgy did not reflect the peace and unity that should characterize the Lord's Supper. Without this, they were only eating "your own supper." Presumably, St. Paul's congregation was duly chastised and resolved to work on peace and unity before their next eucharistic meeting. We prepare to celebrate the eucharistic meal by discerning the Lord's body before, during, and after the assembly's liturgy.

39. "The German Mass and Order of Service," 1526, in *Luther's Works*, 53:84.

40. Martin Luther, *The Small Catechism* 6, in *The Book of Concord*, ed. Theodore G. Tappert et al. (Philadelphia: Fortress, 1959) 352.

2

Karl Barth on the Lord's Supper: An Ecumenical Appraisal

George Hunsinger

As is well known, Karl Barth offered no sustained account of the Lord's Supper in his *Church Dogmatics*. Although such an account was planned, he did not live long enough to write it. It would have appeared in *Church Dogmatics*, volume IV, part 4 after his discussions of baptism and the Lord's Prayer. The material on baptism eventually appeared as IV/4 "Fragment," and an abbreviated discussion of the Lord's Prayer appeared in a separate volume called *The Christian Life*.[1] *The Christian Life* was published posthumously, while the IV/4 "Fragment" appeared shortly before Barth's death.

By the time he was writing volume IV, Barth had come to reject the idea that baptism and the Lord's Supper should be regarded as "sacraments." There was one and only one sacrament, he contended, and that was the mystery of the incarnation itself. Accordingly, baptism and the Lord's Supper should not be regarded as "means of grace," but rather as "responses to grace." They did not have to do with God's actions toward us, but rather with our actions toward God. In the Doctrine of Reconciliation, he concluded, they belonged in the final section concerned with "ethics."

---

1. Karl Barth, *The Christian Life* (Grand Rapids: Eerdmans, 1981).

In the earlier volumes of *Church Dogmatics*, Barth devoted occasional attention here and there to the Lord's Supper. Although these discussions were not sustained, they are still of interest. Prior to volume IV, moreover, he still looked on baptism and the Lord's Supper as sacraments.[2]

The discussion that follows will examine three themes from Barth's earlier and later volumes: the relationship of preaching to the Eucharist, the possible nature of the "sacramental union," and the idea of eucharistic sacrifice.

1

In the early volumes of his *Dogmatics*, Barth argued, in good Reformation fashion, for the priority of the Word over the Sacrament, and therefore for the priority of proclamation over the Lord's Supper in worship. "Real proclamation," he wrote, "is that event in the Church's life which governs all others" (I/1, 88 rev.). It is because of proclamation that the church is a creature of God's Word (*creatura verbum dei*). Through this ongoing event the church receives its very existence. By means of proclamation, the church is, and continually becomes, what it is. It is "continually called and upheld and enlightened and guided by [God's] Word" (III/3, 22). "We have to say that in this event the Church itself must ever and again become the Church" (I/1, 88).

Therefore preaching is "the central part of the Church's liturgy" (I/2, 231). It does something that the sacraments can never do. It represents "the comprehensive and unassailable givenness of revelation itself" (I/2, 231). Being less restricted than the sacraments, preaching represents more fully the whole counsel of God. The purpose of the sacraments is then to illustrate the content of preaching and give it special emphasis. "What applies to proclamation and the Church generally cannot be better illustrated than by the sacrament" (I/1, 88). The earthly elements in the sacrament are "consecrated" and "sanctified" by God's Word in order to "seal" and "confirm" what the Word proclaimes (I/1, 88; I/2, 227). Along these lines Calvin's view is summarized with approval: "[The sacraments] are, so to speak, seal-impressions, or paintings, or reflections of the divine promise of grace; they are supporting pillars of faith, or exercises (*exercitia*) to develop certainty about the Word of God" (I/2, 229).

2. Or at least he had not yet explicitly rejected the idea.

By contrast, the Roman Catholic neglect of preaching, and its reversal of this pattern in favor of the sacraments, is singled out for pointed criticism. According to Catholic teaching, preaching is not strictly necessary. "The Mass may be complete without it" (I/1, 66). For the Catholic Church, Barth wrote, it is "as though preaching did not even exist as an indispensable means of grace" (I/1, 65). Theological discussions about the "teaching office" could proceed in "complete silence about preaching" (I/1, 65). "In sharp distinction from the sacrament," Barth noted, "preaching is not a constitutive element in the Roman Catholic concept of the priesthood" (I/1, 67). Even in the best of cases, the celebration of the sacrament took precedence over the proclamation of the Word. But this method of operating was not without consequences for the Catholic Church, for it led to a certain "poverty" at the center of this "mighty structure" (I/1, 67).

Before turning to examine how Vatican II attempted to correct this situation, a special contribution of the sacrament to preaching, as understood by the earlier Barth, may be noted. At one point Barth went a small step beyond the Reformation when reflecting on John 1:14.

> Ὁ λόγος σάρξ ἐγένετο (John 1:14)—preaching, too, can and must say this. But in a way which preaching can never do, the sacrament underlines the words σάρξ and ἐγένετο. . . . The sacrament's insistence upon this quality in divine sign-giving is its special feature as compared with preaching and its special feature in the whole life of God's people assembled to form the Church. (I/2, 230)

Here the sacrament did not merely confirm, illustrate, or seal the Word of preaching. It palpably attested an essential quality of revelation. For revelation, by definition, involved the giving of signs, and the sacrament manifested this quality in a way that surpassed what preaching could do. The givenness of signs in the sacrament represented, uniquely, the objective aspect of divine revelation.

Roman Catholic teaching since Vatican II offered some redress to Barth's concerns. It made preaching essential to the liturgy though without entirely reversing the traditional priorities.

In the document *Sacrosanctum Concilium* (December 4, 1963), Vatican II affirmed that the Mass was not complete without preaching, at least as far as Sunday worship was concerned:

> 52. By means of the homily the mysteries of the faith and the guiding principles of the Christian life are expounded from the sacred text, during the course of the liturgical year; the homily, therefore,

> is to be highly esteemed as part of the liturgy itself; in fact, at those
> Masses which are celebrated with the assistance of the people on
> Sundays and feasts of obligation, it should not be omitted except
> for a serious reason.

> 56. The two parts which, in a certain sense, go to make up the
> Mass, namely, the Liturgy of the Word and the Eucharistic Liturgy,
> are so closely connected with each other that they form but one
> single act of worship . . .

At the same time, however, the Eucharist retained pride of place. Vatican II
stated explicitly and in various ways the ongoing priority of the sacrament:
"The Eucharist is the source and summit of the Christian life."[3] The eucharistic liturgy still took precedence over the Liturgy of the Word. Moreover,
insofar as "private Masses" were permitted and conducted without the ne-
cessity of preaching, the Mass was still seen as complete without it.

Ecumenically, the result would seem to be a matter of impasse. On
the one hand, we have the Reformational view, represented by Barth, that
preaching is essential for Christian worship and for the very being of the
church, while the Eucharist, though important, would be optional on any
given Sunday (even if required on some regular basis). (The later Barth
urged that it be celebrated every Sunday.) On the other hand, we have the
contemporary Roman Catholic alternative that the Eucharist is always essential, while preaching, though mandatory except under exceptional cir-
cumstances, is still secondary and in principle dispensable.

A way beyond the impasse is suggested by Alexander Schmemann. In
his book *The Eucharist: Sacrament of the Kingdom*, Schmemann posits an
"unbreakable unity of word and sacrament."[4] The word proclaims Christ in
his saving significance as the Incarnate Savior. The sacrament, on the other
hand, is said to do more than merely "confirm" the word and "illustrate" it.
It rather "fulfills" and "interprets" it.

> In the sacrament we partake of him who comes and abides with
> us in the word, and the mission of the Church consists precisely in
> announcing the good news. The word presupposes the sacrament
> as its fulfillment, for in the sacrament Christ the Word becomes
> our life. . . . It is precisely through the sacrament that the word is
> interpreted, for the interpretation of the word is always witness

3. *Lumen Gentium* 11; cf. *Sacrosanctum Concilium* 11–13, 14.

4. *The Eucharist: Sacrament of the Kingdom*, trans. Paul Kachur (Crestwood, NY: St.
Vladimir's Seminary Press, 1988) 69.

> to the fact that the Word has become our life. . . . The sacrament of the word . . . finds its fulfillment and completion in the offering, consecration and distribution to the faithful of the eucharistic gifts.[5]

Schmemann suggests that the separation of the word from the sacrament in the West—whether by emphasizing the word at the expense of the sacrament or the sacrament at the expense of the word—led to "an erroneous, one-sided and distorted understanding of both *word*—i.e., holy scripture and its place in the life of the church—and *sacrament*."[6]

> I daresay that the gradual "decomposition" of scripture, its dissolution in more and more specialized and negative criticism, is a result of its alienation from the eucharist—and practically from the Church herself—as an experience of a spiritual reality. And in its own turn, this same alienation deprived the sacrament of its evangelical content, converting it into a self-contained and self-sufficient "means of sanctification."[7]

When the sacrament is severed from proclamation and so from Scripture, it threatens to become an object of priestly manipulation and superstition. On the other hand, when Scripture is severed from its fulfillment in the sacrament, it all too easily dissolves under the pressures of modern scholarly dissection. Only when word and sacrament are held firmly together in the liturgy, and so in the formative experience of the church, can each truly be what it is.

Although Barth saw no direct way beyond the liturgical impasse as noted here in the Western churches, he nonetheless suggested, at one point, a promising pattern of thought. As I have shown in several places, he often drew upon the logic of the "Chalcedonian pattern" to set forth two terms and their relationship. Abstracting from the famous and authoritative "Chalcedonian Definition," which related the two "natures" of Christ, Barth characteristically drew upon the logic of Chalcedon to elucidate the relationship of other paired terms. Of particular interest in this connection is his discussion of "justification" and "sanctification." With an explicit use of Chalcedonian terminology (quoted repeatedly in the original Greek), Barth explains that these two concepts are best seen as related "without

5. Ibid., 68–69. There is a slight tilt here in favor of the sacrament. For Barth and the Reformation, Christ would already have become our life through the event of preaching.

6. Ibid., 66.

7. Ibid.

separation or division," on the one hand, and "without confusion or change," on the other. The errors that can creep in through either "separating" or "confusing" justification and sanctification are elaborated at some length (IV/2, 499–511).

However, beyond working with the ideas of unity-in-distinction and distinction-in-unity here, as implied by the Chalcedonian pattern— "without separation or division" suggests an inseparable unity, while "without confusion or change" implies an abiding distinction—Barth typically added the idea of an asymmetrical ordering principle (as originally entailed by the fact that in the Person of Christ the divine and the human are not on the same plane). Therefore, one might anticipate that in conclusion Barth would order "justification" clearly over "sanctification," or would he perhaps do the reverse?

In fact, he does neither. Instead he proposes what might be called a "double asymmetry." If we think in terms of "ground" and "consequence," he suggests, then justification would be the ground and sanctification the consequence. The priority and precedence would then belong to justification. However, if we think in terms of "precondition" and "telos," then the pattern would be reversed. Justification would become the precondition while sanctification would be the telos. In that sense the priority would belong to sanctification. "We can and must give the primacy," Barth concluded, "now to the one and now to the other, according to the different standpoints from which we look" (IV/2, 511).

The idea of a double asymmetry can be used to relate word and sacrament. If we adopt the ground/consequence standpoint, the priority would be assigned to the word as the ground so that the sacrament would be seen as the consequence. (This move would be in line with the Reformation.) If, on the other hand, we took the standpoint of precondition/telos, the situation would be much the reverse, with the priority being assigned teleologically to the sacrament for which the word would then serve as the precondition. (This standpoint would comport with Catholicism.) There would be no higher synthesis. Each standpoint would have its relative legitimacy, and each would necessarily complement and supplement the other. The language of "confirmation" would align with the first move, while the language of "fulfillment" would befit the second. Along these lines, I suggest, the western liturgical impasse on this question might find a happy resolution.

2

A much deeper problem for ecumenism concerns the real presence of Christ in the Eucharist, a notoriously vexed question. One popular solution among Protestants is just to affirm Christ's real eucharistic presence while paying no special attention to how his body and blood might be related to the gifts of bread and wine. As attractive as this solution might seem, it unfortunately does nothing to bring the churches closer to visible unity. The question of Christ and the consecrated elements must be tackled directly if eucharistic sharing is ever going to occur where it now fails to exist.

Barth sometimes seemed to adopt the more popular view. He connected the eucharistic "presence" of Christ with his "body and blood" yet without investigating the question of the status of the elements. He could use language about "Christ himself" as though it were simply identical with language about his "body and blood." "In order that others may . . . appropriate what is active and revealed in him," Barth wrote, "he . . . does not offer up anything less than himself, his body and blood: This is my body. And this is my blood" (IV/2, 258). The Lord's Supper meant, Barth explained, that "he will give them his body to eat and his blood to drink. He will give them himself at the cost of his death" (II/2, 474). The Christian was someone who was is baptized into Christ, and who could "receive his body and blood, Jesus Christ Himself, in the Lord's Supper" (III/3, 273). Christ was said to use "the bread and the wine only to signify himself" (II/2, 474).

The idea of "real presence" did not need to be restricted to the Eucharist. Barth reasoned:

> There is obviously no baptism or Lord's Supper without his real presence as very God and very Man, both body and soul. But this presence cannot be regarded as restricted to what were later called the "sacraments." For these are only a symbolical expression of the fact that in its worship the community is gathered directly around Jesus himself, and lives by and with him, of the fact that through faith he rules over the hearts and lives of all even apart from worship. (III/2, 467–68 rev.)

In good Reformed fashion Barth was inclined to focus more on the eucharistic action than on the elements. As the community engaged in the action of eating the bread and drinking the cup, it received Christ, who was really present, along with his benefits.

> The offering of My body and blood has for you the effect that as
> you eat this bread My life is given to you as yours, and that as you
> drink of this cup you may live with joy and not with sorrow, as in-
> nocent and not condemned. . . . Do this ("in remembrance of me")
> as you eat this bread and drink this cup. Proclaim in this way the
> Lord's death until he comes (1 Cor 11:26), i.e., until his presence,
> already experienced here and now with this eating and drinking,
> is revealed to all eyes. (III/2, 214)

The command "Do this in remembrance of me" referred to the disciples'
"sacramental" action of eating and drinking, which in turn meant their
communion in Christ's body and blood. "Real presence" was a matter of his
action in their action.

> And that is why the eucharistic action as the crowning act of wor-
> ship—τοῦτο, this, i.e., the common eating and drinking of the dis-
> ciples according to his command—is no more and no less than his
> body and blood. . . . This action then, accomplished εἰς τὴν ἐμὴν
> ἀνάμνησιν [in remembrance of me], is the direct proclamation of
> his death until he comes (1 Cor 11:26). In this provisional form as
> the action of the community, it is his own action, the work of his
> real presence. Here and now he himself is for them—his offered
> body and his shed blood—the communion of saints thanking and
> confessing him in this action. (IV/2, 658)

Barth had little patience for "complicated arguments as to the precise nature of the bread and wine" (III/2, 502). The closest he came to reflecting
directly on their special eucharistic status—apart from passing remarks like
saying they are sanctified by the Word (I/1, 89)—took place when he considered the concept of "sacramental union." As was perhaps to be expected,
Barth examined this idea only to reject it.

Barth's main concern was that the "hypostatic union" (*unio hypostatica*) was something *sui generis*, in other words, in a category by itself
(IV/2, 37, 52). It was irreducibly singular and absolutely unique. It could
have no true analogies. Not even the idea of a "sacramental union" (*unio
sacramentalis*)—a term found not only in Luther and the Lutheran confessions, but also (as Barth fails to note) in Reformed theologians like Vermigli,
Bucer, Cranmer, and occasionally Calvin—could serve as a proper parallel
(IV/2, 54–55). The incarnation itself, Barth insisted, represented the only
possible "sacramental union," because, according to his later thinking, the
incarnation was itself "the one and only sacrament" (IV/2, 55). The idea of
a sacramental union between Christ's life-giving flesh and the eucharistic

elements led in the end, Barth warned, to the impossible Roman Catholic view that the church was a prolongation of the incarnation (*incarnatus prolognatus*). The incarnation, Barth argued, allowed for no "repeated actualization" (*wiederholten Verwirklichung*) of itself—no "representation and repetition": not in the sacramental union and not in the being of church (IV/2, 55).

A similar point was made regarding imagery. Because the mystery of the incarnation was incomparable by definition, none of the traditional images for it could withstand scrutiny.

> Absolute caution is needed in respect of comparisons like the following—that the Word is in flesh like a man in his clothes, or a sailor in his boat, or glowing and heat and light in iron. The fathers occasionally used pictures like this, and they have a passing value by way of illustration. But it must not be overlooked how incongruent they really are. We have to realize that the being of the Son of God in human art and kind is not really like the external association of two realities like a man and his clothes or a sailor and his boat, nor like the relationship between a substance like iron and its properties of glowing and heat and light, so that it has no real analogies in the proportions of these relationships. (IV/2, 53)

The care with which Barth frames these reflections is not to be missed. Because the incarnation has "no real analogies," "absolute caution" is needed in making any "comparisons" to it. All images and examples are finally "incongruent." Nevertheless, pictures may occasionally be used as long as it is recognized that they have only "passing value" by way of "illustration." Illustrations are therefore not absolutely ruled out if used with the proper caution.

A salient difference emerges at this point between dogmatic theology and ecumenical theology. Dogmatic theology seeks to determine what is doctrinally correct, as seen from a particular confessional standpoint. Once that determination has been made, the task is to defend it against any conflicting positions that may be found in other confessional traditions. When these conflicting positions are "church-dividing," however, so that the divided churches can no longer engage in eucharistic sharing, then ecumenical theology must go beyond dogmatic theology. It must strive to achieve sufficient "convergence" (not necessarily consensus) that the obstacles to eucharistic sharing are mitigated and overcome. As I have argued elsewhere, while no tradition can be expected to compromise on essentials, false contrasts need to be overcome, and every step toward confessional convergence must be taken that can be taken without theological compromise.[8]

As I have argued at length in *The Eucharist and Ecumenism*, if Protestants today were to embrace something like the Eastern Orthodox view of *unio sacramentalis*, as actually happened to varying degrees during the Reformation—not only among the Lutherans but also among the Reformed (particularly Vermigli, Bucer, and Cranmer)—then to that extent a major step would be taken toward ecumenical healing and convergence.

Although Barth discussed the patristic image of the iron in the fire, he considered it only in relation to the *unio hypostatica* but not in relation to the *unio sacramentalis* (IV/2, 53, 66). In Eastern Orthodoxy, however, beginning with the patristic period, the image of the iron in the fire was used as an illustration for both forms of union. In the 16th century this usage was then picked up, in various ways, by both Lutheran and Reformed theologians to illustrate the *unio sacramentalis* (and among the Lutherans also the *unio hypostatica*).[9]

Barth is of course correct that the mystery of the incarnation is incomparable so that no proper analogy or illustration can be found for it. All suggested analogies or illustrations can only be flawed and incongruous. A total ban against them for that reason, however, would seem to be overly severe. In another connection Barth himself would cite Hilary of Poitiers: *Non sermoni res, sed rei sermo subjectus est* (I/1, 354).[10] "The thing itself is not subject to the word, but the word to the thing." Or perhaps better: "The subject matter is not subordinate to the language, but the language to the subject matter." In other words, the language needs to be interpreted in light of the theological content to which it refers, and not the reverse. Therefore, as long as certain analogies or illustrations are kept under theological control, so that their limitations are clearly recognized, there would seem to be no good reason not to use them with all due caution.

The image of the iron in the fire has obvious limitations for both the *unio hypostatica* and the *unio sacramentalis*. Because the image is impersonal and mechanical, and because each of the unions in itself is incomparable,

---

8. George Hunsinger, *The Eucharist and Ecumenism: Let Us Keep the Feast* (Cambridge: Cambridge University Press, 2008) 9–10.

9. Ibid., 41–46.

10. Hilary of Poitiers, *On the Trinity* IV.14, in *Nicene and Post-Nicene Fathers*, Series 2, ed. Philip Schaff (Grand Rapids: Eerdmans, 1983) 9:75.

Hilary's rule would have to apply: *Non sermoni res, sed rei sermo subjectus est.* Nevertheless, in certain respects the iron-in-the-fire image is not a bad device for illustrating what is at stake in certain applications of the Chalcedon pattern. The picture of a red-hot iron glowing in the fire captures at least three important elements: unity ("without separation or division"), distinction ("without confusion or change"), and an ordering principle of priority or precedence (asymmetry). As the fire suffuses the iron, the two enter into a kind of mutual participation (unity). Nevertheless, the iron remains iron, even as the fire remains fire; neither disappears into the other (distinction). At the same time, the fire retains a kind of priority or precedence over the iron; the fire may be conceived as transcending the iron that rests in it (asymmetry). If not too much weight is put on it, the illustration would seem to be of tolerable and passing value.

It is worth noting that Barth did not always shy away from using the image himself. "Red-hot iron burns," he once wrote, "not because by its nature it possesses burning activity, but because it has acquired the latter through its union with the fire" (I/2, 137). This was stated in illustration of the *unio hypostatica*, or more specifically, of how, in the incarnation, the "flesh" is related to the "Word" as the iron is related to the fire (John 1:14).

With this illustration in mind, let me try to lay out how I see the analogy between the hypostatic union and the sacramental union. I see it as an analogy of proportion: A is to B as C is to D. The first two terms have a relationship to each other similar to that which the second two have to each other. The similarity holds true in spite of the differences in the two relationships.

With regard to the hypostatic union, A is divine and B is human. The two terms are therefore radically different. God, who is not an object in the universe, belongs to no genus, but the human nature of Jesus belongs to a genus in the creation. Mark McIntosh puts their relationship nicely. The divine and human "natures" are united, he says, in the Person of the Son, who enacts them in a living unity. In his Person, I would add, the two natures enjoy a dynamic oneness, what the tradition calls *communio naturarum*. I would interpret this idea, in the first instance, as a living communion of the two natures.

By living communion, I mean that in his divine nature the Son acts in and through his human nature, and that in his human nature he operates receptively in and through his divine nature. It is the Son who acts, not the natures, but in him the natures are not static. They rather coinhere in a mysterious dynamism. This living communion, like all forms of theological communion, is governed, I would say, by the Chalcedonian pattern. The divine and human natures are hypostasized in the Son "without separation or division," "without confusion or change," and with an "asymmetrical" priority of the divine over the human. The human nature is assumed into union with the Person of the Son so that, through him as the personal acting subject, it enters into concert with his divine nature.

Two corollaries would follow from this analysis. One pertains to suffering and death, the other to exaltation and transfiguration. These are of course complicated questions. Here I must be brief. As to the first, I would say that through his divine nature the eternal Son suffers and dies in his human nature. His suffering and death are therefore incomprehensible but real. Through his incarnation the Son enters fully into suffering and death without ceasing to be the impassible and immortal God. The inconceivablity of this humiliation seems be what Cyril had in mind when he stated that the Son "suffered impassibly" and "died immortally."[11]

The second corollary is much the reverse. Through his divine nature the Incarnate Son elevates his human nature into a glorified and immortal final state. His human nature, while it does not cease to be finite and fully human, is inconceivably exalted into a new, "divinized" form. It is the splendorous form that was unveiled on the mount of transfiguration, and while now hidden to us in the time between the times, it is fully enjoyed by him in heaven, even as it will be universally manifested at the end of all things. The inconceivability of this exaltation seems *in optimem partem* to be what Gregory of Nyssa and other Eastern Fathers meant when they wrote about the "transelementation" of Christ's human flesh.[12]

This dynamic coinherence of divine and human natures in the action, passion and exaltation of the Incarnate Son is what I take to be the *communio naturarum*. In short, the *communio naturarum* is a form of *koinonia*, anchored and actualized in the Person of the Word made flesh, and governed formally by the Chalcedonian pattern.[13]

11. See Paul L. Gavrilyuk, *The Suffering of the Impassible God: The Dialectics of Patristic Thought* (Oxford: Oxford University Press, 2004) 135–75.

12. Despite certain problems in some of their expressions of it. See Donald Fairbairn, "Patristic Soteriology: Three Trajectories," *Journal of the Evangelical Theological Society* 50 (2007) 289–310.

13. In these formulations I have tried to follow the outlook of the Reformed tradition as set forth by Barth. While not rejecting the *communio naturarum*, Barth anchors it in the *unio hypostatica*, "giving priority and precedence to the doctrine of the *unio*

Turning to the sacramental union, on the other hand, the two terms—Christ's flesh and the sacramental elements—both belong, respectively, to one or another genus in the creation. In that sense they differ not in essence but in mode. Through the presiding eucharistic minister, the risen and ascended Son, in the *epiclesis* of the Spirit, unites his life-giving flesh with the gifts of bread and wine. The gifts are inconceivably elevated, transformed and offered in a new mystical or sacramental mode of being. Just as in the hypostatic union the Son's flesh exists in his Person in dynamic union with his deity, so also in the sacramental union the elements come to exist no longer in their pre-consecrated state, but in a mysterious superabundance with Christ's life-giving flesh. Without ceasing to be bread and wine, they are made one with his glorified flesh so that by means of them the Son will unite the faithful to himself through his body and blood. I take this mystical transformation and union to be what Vermigli, following Theophylact, meant by "transelementation." The bread and wine are transelemented in order that through them, succinctly put, the faithful themselves might be transelemented into Christ.

Again, we have a pattern of dynamic coinherence. Christ's flesh dwells in the elements, and the elements dwell in his flesh, through a type of asymmetrical union: without separation or division, without confusion or change, and with priority and precedence belonging throughout to Christ's flesh, or better, to the living Christ under the aspect of his flesh. "The bread that we break, is it not a participation [*koinonia*] in the body of Christ?" (1 Cor 10:16). The quality of *koinonia*—regarded as a dynamic, differentiated and asymmetrical form of reciprocal participation—is the common element in both the hypostatic and the sacramental unions.[14]

Despite all differences, the common quality of *koinonia* is, in effect, what allowed the early Greek Fathers to apply the image of the iron in the fire to both the sacramental and the hypostatic unions. As McIntosh eloquently suggests: "The bread is more bread than ever, more deeply Food, more profoundly the means of Communion, precisely by being the Body of Christ; the very trajectory of its creaturely 'nature' is not abrogated but supereminently consummated as Christ releases it into his own life."[15]

---

hypostatica over that of the *communio naturarum*" (IV/2, 66; cf. 68).

14. See Martin Luther, *The Babylonian Captivity of the Church*, in *Luther's Works*, American ed. (Philadelphia: Fortress, 1959) 36:34. At this point Luther interprets the sacramental union, as implied by 1 Cor 10:16, in analogy with the hypostatic union.

15. Mark McIntosh, "Christ the Word Who Makes Us: Eucharist and Creation," *Pro Ecclesia* 19 (2010) 255–59, at 259.

This explanation of the analogy between the two unions is meant to clarify how "transelementation" might be understood in relation to the incarnation. The formal terms of the analogy could be restated, in light of this analysis, more precisely as: B is to A as C is to B', where B stands for Christ's human nature, A for his divine nature, C for the consecrated elements and B' for Christ's glorified, life-giving flesh (or more precisely, for the incarnate Word under the aspect of his life-giving flesh). The *koinonia* relation of B to A is similar to that between C and B.

Other traditions might wish to offer different interpretations of eucharistic conversion. My claims are meant to be modest. This view of transelementation, I suggest, could be adopted without compromise by the Reformed; and if it were, it would not be church-dividing. Although far from anything found in Barth, it does not seem incompatible with much that he affirmed. It tries to take his dogmatic convictions seriously while moving them in a more ecumenical direction.

3

Barth arguably failed to exploit the full potential of his theology regarding the Eucharist. One statement in particular helps to make this failing clear. In the midst of a fine comment on the Lord's Supper, he distances himself from the Roman Catholic mass. The Eucharist is not to be seen, he says, as "a re-presentation and repetition" of Christ's sacrifice—"as in the Romanist doctrine of the Mass"—but rather as "a simple and full enjoyment of its benefits," and in particular of "the eternal life won for us in him" (III/2, 502).[16]

From the standpoint of Barth's theology, this is an odd comment. It reflects standard Reformation polemic more than his own best insights. It not only conflates re-presentation unnecessarily with repetition, but also divorces Christ from his benefits. These are two moves, however, that Barth has taught us to avoid.[17]

16. Note that this remark was penned in 1948, well before the emergence of anything like Vatican II. Moreover, by "re-presentation" what Barth had in mind was probably something sacerdotal, not something effected by the living Christ himself.

17. Nevertheless, it was Barth's considerd judgment. "There can be no question of any repetition or representation of that event, or even of an actualisation which has still to be effected. It needs no completion or re-presentation" (IV/1, 295). It is "impossible to make what took place ἐφ' ἅπαξ in Jesus Christ coincident with what takes place in faith" (IV/1, 767). "The most questionable feature of the Roman Mass" is "its character

First, Barth knew that Christ could not be enjoyed without his benefits, and that the reverse was also true, namely, that his benefits were unavailable without his person. Christ's benefits could be enjoyed only by way of *participatio Christi*. Moreover, Barth also knew that Christ's person was inseparable from his work, so that where Christ was present, his saving work was present as well. Humankind was not saved by the work of Christ *in abstracto*, Barth held, so much as by the person of Christ in his work. A separation of Christ's work of sacrifice on the cross from its benefits, as though the sacrifice were merely past while the benefits alone were present fails to correspond with Barth's best insights. The very being of Christ was in his saving actions. Christ's sacrificial work on the cross belonged inseparably to his being as a person. His sacrificial work had no benefit that could be enjoyed apart from his person to which both the work and the benefit belonged.

Second, the idea that the being of Christ was in his work, and the work of Christ in his being, committed Barth to a doctrine of "re-presentation." Regardless of what one calls it (and it is not easy to find a satisfactory term), it is the actualistic idea that Christ's being in act involves a perfect work (*opere perfectus*) that is also a perpetual operation (*operatione perpetuum*).[18] The perpetual operation adds nothing new in content to the perfect work, which by definition needs no completion. Yet it belongs to the perfect work's perfection that it is not merely encapsulated in the past. On the contrary, it operates perpetually to make itself present for what it is, again and again. Barth explained:

> In God's revelation, which is the content of His Word, we have in fact to do with His act. And first, this means generally—with an event, with a happening. But as such this is an event which is in no sense to be transcended. It is not, therefore, an event which has merely happened and is now a past fact of history. God's revelation is, of course, this as well. But it is also an event happening in the present, here and now. Again, it is not this in such a way that it exhausts itself in the momentary movement from the past to the present, that is, in our to-day. But it is also an event that took place once for all, and an accomplished fact. And it is also future—the

---

as a representation of the sacrifice of Golgotha" (IV/3, 395). Barth (mistakenly) saw the Roman Catholic view of the Mass as involving a "new sacrifice" (IV/2, 640).

18. Barth first used these terms, which he borrowed from Quenstedt, in his classroom lectures from 1924, which were posthumously published as Barth, *Unterricht in der christlichen Religion* (Zürich: Theologischer Verlag, 1985) 148. See also I/1, 427.

event which lies completely and wholly in front of us, which has
not yet happened, but which simply comes upon us. Again, this
happens without detriment to its historical completeness and its
full contemporaneity. (II/1, 262)

The event of Jesus Christ, Barth suggested, is not only "a past fact of history," but also "an event that is happening in the present here and now."
Furthermore, "in its historical completeness" and "full contemporaneity,"
is it is also an event that is "truly future." The past-tense form of this un-
transcendable event is definitive and constitutive, its future-tense form is
final and unsurpassable, while its present-tense form is at once secondary
and derivative (with respect to its past) and yet also anticipatory and provi-
sional (with respect to its future).

The full contemporaneity of Christ's person in his work here and now,
and of his work in his person, would have to take place, at least for the
earlier Barth, primarily through Word and Sacrament. Yet it fell to T. F. Torrance, Barth's student, to make the connection that his mentor never quite
managed to carry through: "The action of the Supper," wrote Torrance, "is
not another action than that which Christ has already accomplished on our
behalf, and which is proclaimed in the Gospel."[19] It is rather the very same
action in a new and sacramental form.[20] Ecumenical theology after Barth
has every reason to exploit this insight.

According to Geoffrey Wainwright, eucharistic sacrifice "is likely to
be the area of greatest difficulty for classical Protestants on the way to an
ecumenical Eucharist."[21] Protestants, he notes, "are still likely to balk at the
idea from Vatican II that the Church or the faithful 'offer the divine vic-
tim to God.'"[22] "Clearly," he continues, "there is still theological work to be
done towards an ecumenical Eucharist in so far as its sacrificial nature is
at stake."[23] Wainwright even states that eucharistic sacrifice may be a more

19. Thomas F. Torrance, *Conflict and Agreement in the Church* (London: Lutterworth,
1960) 2:152.

20. Just as Barth could write about the "threefold parousia," or one parousia in three
very different temporal forms (IV/3, 292–96, 755, 794), so also is it possible to conceive
of Christ's "threefold saving sacrifice," or his one saving sacrifice in three very different
temporal forms, as is explained more fully below. The intermediate form would be the
Eucharist.

21. Geoffrey Wainwright, "*Ecclesia de Eucharistia vivit*: An Ecumenical Reading,"
Ecumenical Trends 33 (2004) 129–37, at 132.

22. Ibid., 133.

23. Ibid.

difficult problem to solve than that of eucharistic ministry: "I would suggest that settlement of the meaning of eucharistic sacrifice is logically prior to the question of the disabling 'defectus' which Vatican II's Decree on Ecumenism alleges in the ministry of those who preside at the Lord's Table in the Protestant churches."[24]

Wainwright does not elaborate on the barriers to a settlement with classical Protestantism. Obviously, they are mainly two: first, that the sacrifice of Calvary is unrepeatable; and second, that the Eucharist is not a meritorious work. Can the Eucharist be understood as a "sacrifice" in a way that honors the unrepeatability of Christ's once-for-all sacrifice on the cross? Furthermore, can it be conceived as a "sacrifice" in a way that prevents it from functioning as a "meritorious work"? The first of these questions will be considered here, with reference to the to the work of Torrance.[25]

Torrance's contribution of to the question of eucharistic sacrifice is at least threefold. He developed an integrated conception of Christ's person and work, he showed how the cross and the Eucharist can be held together in a pattern of unity-in-distinction, and he explained how Christ's vicarious humanity allows *participatio Christi* to be grounded in grace alone. In addition, he also connected eucharistic sacrifice with Christ's ascension.

First, Torrance developed an integrated conception of Christ's person and work. The person of Christ, he explained, cannot be separated from his work, nor his work from his person, because "his person and his work are one."[26] As the Incarnate Son, Christ "confronts us as he in whom person and word and work are indissolubly one. It is his own person that he communicates in his words and deeds, while his words and deeds do not only derive from his person but inhere in it."[27]

As Christ's person and work are one, so also are his incarnation and atonement. The two are necessarily inseparable and mutually implicated in each other. For Torrance, as for the great patristic theologians on whom he relies, like Athanasius and Cyril, the incarnation reaches its fulfillment in the atonement, while the atonement finds its essential premise in the

24. Ibid., 134.

25. Both questions are considered at greater length in my book *The Eucharist and Ecumenism* (Cambridge: Cambridge University Press, 2008), from which the material in this essay has been excerpted.

26. Thomas F. Torrance, *The Mediation of Christ* (Colorado Springs, CO: Helmers & Howard, 1992) 63.

27. Thomas F. Torrance, *Space, Time and Resurrection* (Grand Rapids: Eerdmans, 1976) 48.

incarnation. That was the point of Torrance's insight that we are not saved by the death of Christ, but by the person of Christ in his death.

Torrance's second contribution was to show how the cross and the Eucharist are held in a unity that does not violate but reinforces their distinction. The one perfect and indivisible act of Atonement in Jesus Christ assumes two different forms. The constitutive form is the cross while the mediating form is the Eucharist. The cross is always central, constitutive and definitive while the Eucharist is always secondary, relative and derivative. The eucharistic form of the one sacrifice does not repeat the unrepeatable, but it does attest what it mediates and mediate what it attests. What it mediates and attests is the one whole Jesus Christ, who in his body and blood is both the sacrifice and the sacrament in one. As the sacrifice, he is the Offerer and the Offering. As the sacrament, he is the Giver and the Gift. The Son's sacrificial offering of himself to the Father for us on the cross is the ground of the Father's sacramental gift of his Son to the faithful in the Eucharist.

The cross was styled by Torrance as the "dimension of depth" in the Eucharist.[28] The Eucharist has no significance in itself that is not derived from the cross and grounded in it. Therefore the cross alone is the saving "content, reality and power" of the Eucharist.[29] It is a matter of one reality, one priestly sacrifice of Christ, in two different temporal forms. The eucharistic form here and now participates in, manifests, and attests the incarnational form of the sacrifice there and then. What took place in the perfect tense is finished, indivisible and all-sufficient. What takes place in the eucharistic sacrifice is not a matter of repetition but of participation, manifestation and witness.

Mention may be made, thirdly, of a further contribution, namely, Torrance's idea of Christ's vicarious humanity. Christ himself, Torrance proposed, functions vicariously as our human response to God. It is by grace through faith that the faithful are given to participate in Christ's perfect human offering of himself to God. Eucharistic mediation and participation provide an answer to the question of repetition that so worried the Reformers. These ideas also address the problem of the mass as a meritorious work. In the Eucharist the living Christ re-presents himself in his

28. See George Hunsinger, "The Dimension of Depth: Thomas F. Torrance on the Sacraments of Baptism and the Lord's Supper," *Scottish Journal of Theology* 54 (2001) 155–76.

29. Thomas F. Torrance, *Theology in Reconciliation: Essays towards Evangelical and Catholic Unity in East and West* (Grand Rapids: Eerdmans, 1975) 82.

vicarious humanity—that is, in his body and blood—so that the faithful are given an active though secondary and derivative participation in it. Recall Calvin's view that it is in and through the priesthood of Christ that we "offer ourselves and all that we are to God."[30] Torrance has shown that there is no reason why this, the self-offering of the faithful, should not be given a eucharistic location.

Finally, like Calvin and the general Reformed tradition, Torrance developed the idea of Christ's ascension. Unlike them, however, and in particular unlike Barth, he applied it to the question of eucharistic sacrifice. Torrance distinguished three aspects of Christ's priestly office in his ascension: his eternal self-offering, his perpetual intercession, and his continual benediction.[31] These will be discussed, briefly, in reverse order. According to Torrance:

> (i) The ascended Christ's eternal benediction is his sending of his Spirit. It is this gift that creates union and communion with Christ. Through this benediction the faithful *live no longer for themselves but for him who for their sakes died and was raised* (2 Cor 5:15).

> (ii) The ascended Christ's perpetual intercession, in turn, is his continual prayer before the Father. By his Spirit he takes up the church's prayers into his own continual intercession, where they are purified and perfected. Because Christ's being is in his act, however, his perpetual intercession is finally inseparable from his person. His perpetual intercession and his eternal self-offering are one.

> (iii) Finally, the ascended Christ's eternal self-offering provides a basis for understanding eucharistic sacrifice. Christ's priestly sacrifice and oblation of himself are multifaceted. In one sense they are necessarily over and done with. But "in their once for all completion," noted Torrance, "they are taken up eternally into the life of God and remain prevalent, efficacious, valid, [and] abidingly real."[32] Christ's historical self-offering on Calvary has taken place once-for-all and needs no repetition. But since the Offerer and the Offering are inherently one, Christ's atoning sacrifice is taken up, through his resurrection and ascension, into the eternal

---

30. *Institutes*, II.15.6.

31. Torrance, *Space, Time and Resurrection*, 115–18.

32. Ibid., 115.

presence of the Father. His self-offering "endures for ever as the one, perfect, sufficient sacrifice for the sins of the world."[33]

The Eucharist must be seen to have a twofold aspect. It involves both communion and sacrifice. "Eucharistic sacrifice means that we *through the Spirit* are so intimately united to Christ, by his body and blood, that we participate in his self-consecration and self-offering to the Father."[34] "It is his one sufficient and once for all offering of himself for us that is our only sacrifice before God."[35] "What we do as we gather together in Christ's name is to offer Christ to the Father, for he who has united us to himself has gathered up and sanctified all our worship and prayer in himself."[36]

There is therefore one sacrifice common to Christ and his church—that is the high point of Torrance's teaching. What he says about the Eucharist runs parallel to what he said in another place, following Athanasius, about baptism, namely, that there is "one baptism common to Christ and his Church."[37] "Because he is baptized," wrote Athanasius, "it is we who are baptized in him."[38] The baptism of the faithful is not another or separate baptism alongside the baptism of Christ. It is rather a participation in his one vicarious baptism as undergone for their sakes. Just as Christ's baptism is vicarious, encompassing and inclusive, so the same is also true of his atoning sacrifice on the cross. The sacrifice of thanks and praise that is offered by the faithful in the Eucharist is taken up into the one atoning sacrifice of Christ, enacted on their behalf. His completed and perpetual self-offering, as sacramentally re-presented in the Eucharist, serves as their means of eternal access to the Father of all mercy and righteousness.

The sacrifice common to Christ and his church is seen as one sacrifice in three modes:

(i) the once-for-all and historical mode in which the work of expiation was completed;

(ii) the ascended and eternal mode by which its efficacy never ends;

33. Torrance, *Theology in Reconciliation*, 133.

34. Ibid., 134.

35. Torrance, *Space, Time and Resurrection*, 117.

36. Torrance, *Theology in Reconciliation*, 212.

37. "The One Baptism Common to Christ and His Church," in ibid., 82–105, at 83.

38. Athanasius, *Oration Against the Arians* I.48, in *Athanasius*, ed. Kahled Anatolios (London: Routledge, 2004) 106.

(iii) the daily and eucharistic mode through which the faithful
come to dwell in Christ and he in them as his sacrifice continually
becomes theirs and theirs his.

While these different modes remain truly distinct, they also form an inseparable unity. It is the unity of a single great sacrifice. It was once accomplished on the cross, then elevated in its efficacy to eternity, on which
basis it is re-presented in the Word and by the Spirit for daily participation,
reception and acknowledgment by the church. The sacramental means for
this daily participation, reception and acknowledgment is the Eucharist as
communion and sacrifice.

4

Three questions about the Eucharist have been examined in this essay: (i)
how preaching and the Eucharist are related in Christian worship, (ii) how
the *unio hypostatica* might be related to the *unio sacramentalis*, and (iii)
how Christ's sacrifice on Calvary might be related to the eucharistic sacrifice. On the first question, a resolution was proposed through the grammar
of a "double asymmetry," as derived from a suggestion of Barth's. From one
standpoint the priority and precedence would belong to preaching; from
another it would belong to the Eucharist. The second question moved
toward ecumenical convergence by applying the logic of the "Chalcedonian pattern," as again derived from Barth's writings. Applied beyond and
against him, the pattern established a basis for seeing the hypostatic and the
sacramental unions as analogous examples of *koinonia* relations, despite
their irreducible differences. Finally, on the basis of Barth's "actualism," but
against his considered judgment, a proposal was sketched to explain how
eucharistic sacrifice could be affirmed without compromise by a theology
rooted in the Reformation, and in particular in the Reformed tradition. The
once-for-all sacrifice of Calvary was seen as involving a perpetual operation
that allowed for its continual eucharistic self-actualization. In these and
other ways, Barth's great dogmatic achievement, it was suggested, allows
for fruitful ecumenical extensions.

Liturgical Postscript

Are there any precedents for the Reformed churches in particular, and the Protestant churches in general, that could be drawn upon for guidance in incorporating the theme of eucharistic sacrifice into their liturgies? A few prayers and hymns may be noted.

A liturgy from the Church of Scotland (1957) includes this eucharistic prayer:

> We bless you for his continual intercession and rule at your right hand, . . . and pleading his eternal sacrifice, we your servants set forth this memorial which he has commanded us to make.[39]

In a prayer from the Scottish Episcopal Church (1982), the theme of union with Christ is brought out more directly:

> Made one with him, we offer you these gifts and with them ourselves, a single, holy, living sacrifice.[40]

Christ's once-for-all sacrifice, its perpetual efficacy, and its eucharistic availability through the Holy Spirit, all receive fine expression in this prayer from the Church of England Liturgical Commission (ca. 1985):

> Father, as we plead his sacrifice made once for all on the cross , we remember his dying and rising to glory, and rejoice that he prays for us at your right hand: pour out your Holy Spirit over us and these gifts, which we bring before you from your own creation; show them to be for us the body and blood of your dear Son; unite in his eternal sacrifice all who share the food and drink of his new and unending life.[41]

Turning from prayers to hymns, an astonishing number by Charles Wesley have been collected by J. Ernest Rattenbury.[42] For Victorian beauty

---

39. Cited in Max Thurian, *Eucharistic Memorial*, trans. J. G. Davies (London: Lutterworth, 1960) 2:106 n. 61. Here lightly edited.

40. Cited in Kenneth Stevenson, "Eucharistic Sacrifice: What Can We Learn from Christian Antiquity?" in *Essays on Eucharistic Sacrifice in the Early Church*, ed. Colin Buchanan (Bramcote Notts: Grove, 1984) 26–33, at 32n.

41. Cited in Bryan D. Spinks, "The Ascension and Vicarious Humanity of Christ," in *Time and Community*, ed. J. Neil Alexander (Washington, DC: Pastoral, 1990) 185–201, at 201 n. 83.

42. J. Ernest Rattenbury, *The Eucharistic Hymns of John and Charles Wesley* (Cleveland: Order of St. Luke, 1990).

and the keen spirit of the Reformation, however, William Bright's great hymn of 1874 is unsurpassed and provides a fitting note on which to end:

> And now, O Father, mindful of the love
> that bought us, once for all, on Calvary's Tree,
> and having with us him that pleads above,
> we here present, we spread forth to thee
> that only Offering perfect in thine eyes,
> the one, true, pure, immortal Sacrifice.
>
> Look, Father, look on his anointed face,
> and only look on us as found in him;
> look not on our misusings of thy grace,
> our prayer so languid, and our faith so dim:
> for lo, between our sins and their reward
> we set the Passion of thy Son our Lord.
>
> And so we come: O draw us to thy feet,
> most patient Savior, who canst love us still;
> and by this food, so aweful and so sweet,
> deliver us from every touch of ill:
> in thine own service make us glad and free,
> and grant us never more to part with thee.

3

The Eucharistic Presence of Christ

Bruce D. Marshall

Where We Are

OVER THE LAST FIFTY years or so the real presence of Christ in the Eucharist has become an ecumenical commonplace. Since the sixteenth century the Christian world had seemed divided between two sharply opposed convictions about Christ's eucharistic presence. On the one hand there were those Christian communities, mostly Catholic and Orthodox, which affirmed that Christ's actual body and blood are mysteriously but truly present where the consecrated elements of the Eucharist are present. On the other hand there were those communities, mostly Protestant, which denied any such presence and regarded the earthly elements of the Eucharist as a sign or reminder of Christ's body and blood really present elsewhere, in heaven at the right hand of God. Now these communities, at least as their beliefs are interpreted by official representatives, typically hold that they are a good deal closer on the Eucharist than they had once thought.

Protestants will now often say that their historic insistence on the "spiritual" rather than "carnal" or "physical" character of Christ's eucharistic presence was never meant to deny the reality of that presence. Catholics will now often grant that the traditional Protestant antipathy towards transubstantiation should not be equated with a denial of Christ's real presence in the Eucharist. Protestant theologians are now less likely to defend a purely memorialist or symbolic understanding of the Lord's Supper than they were a generation or two ago, and in traditions where such views were once common, authoritative figures—Calvin, for example—are now interpreted as opposed to any such understanding.

With this has gone a noticeable shift in piety. At the Methodist theology school where I teach, for example, few students are willing to deny outright that what the communicant receives in the Lord's Supper is really the body and blood of Christ, and the memorialist character of historic American Methodist piety is seen as a betrayal of the eucharistic realism of the Wesleys, an unfortunate virus contracted from the Reformed when Methodism emigrated to America.

To be sure, the message has not reached every corner of American Christianity (I can't speak with much knowledge of other parts of the world). There remain those who are convinced that Catholics endanger their souls by "worshipping the wafer god," to recall the language of an illustrated tract I found lying in the dirt outside my parish after Mass a few years ago. But at least in those traditions whose attitudes toward the Eucharist were shaped by substantive theological debate with traditions assumed to oppose their own, the real presence is now widely assumed.

Yet growth in agreement about the reality of Christ's presence in the Eucharist has been accompanied by a striking loss of interest in how to understand that reality. The fact of Christ's presence is now affirmed across old lines of division, but speculation on the way in which Christ is present, on just how it is that this remarkable fact obtains, is not only far less common than it once was, but is often viewed as an obstacle to ecumenical agreement about the fact itself. As it is often put, *that* Christ is present is one thing, *how* he is present another. Ecumenical agreement obtains on the fact, but not on how to understand it. This, however, is no great loss: agreement on the "how" is not necessary for genuine agreement on the fact, so we need not linger in search of it.

The American Lutheran/Roman Catholic dialogue, for example, in an early and influential agreed statement of the Eucharist from 1967, characterizes the result of its discussions like this: "[T]here is agreement on the 'that,' the full reality of Christ's presence. What has been disputed is a particular way of stating the 'how,' the manner in which he becomes present." The "particular way" of understanding Christ's presence to which the dialogue refers is the Catholic teaching on transubstantiation. But discussion with their Catholic partners and a reading of "contemporary Catholic theologians" (specifically the Rahner and Schillebeeckx of the immediate post-conciliar period) has convinced the Lutheran members of the dialogue that "the dogma of transubstantiation intends to affirm the fact of Christ's presence. . .and is not an attempt to explain how Christ becomes present." So understood, Lutherans "must acknowledge that it is a legitimate way of attempting to express the mystery," even though it is one they themselves have good reasons for "prefer[ing] to avoid."[1]

Some years later the Lutheran-Roman Catholic dialogue in Germany (more properly the *Ökumenischer Arbeitskreis evangelischer und katholischer Theologen*, which includes Reformed as well as Lutheran Protestants) reached a conclusion quite similar to its American counterpart: "[T]he emphasis is on the fact of the personal presence of the living Lord in the event of the memorial and fellowship meal, not on the question as to how this real presence, the 'is,' is to be explained."[2]

The approach of these Lutheran/Catholic dialogues is not, I think, exceptional, but became the typical pattern for thinking about eucharistic presence both within and across the various Western traditions. Regarding the precise manner of Christ's real presence in the Eucharist a legitimate plurality of views is on offer, and to insist that one of these, or some of them, are preferable to the others is to threaten the hard-won and far more important agreement on the real presence itself. Better, it generally seems to be assumed, to let the matter alone. Indeed, it seems pointless to pursue a detailed theological understanding of the way in which Christ is present in the consecrated bread and wine, if one already knows in advance that the results of one's labors will in principle be no better than the quite different, even contradictory, results someone else may obtain.

---

1. "The Eucharist: A Lutheran-Roman Catholic Statement," in *Lutherans and Catholics in Dialogue III: The Eucharist as Sacrifice*, ed. Paul C. Empie and T. Austin Murphy (Minneapolis: Augsburg, n.d. [1967]) 196.

2. Karl Lehmann and Wolfhart Pannenberg, eds., *The Condemnations of the Reformation Era: Do They Still Divide?*, trans. Margaret Kohl (Minneapolis: Fortress, 1990) 92; cf. 101, which contrasts "the clear and unambiguous confession of the real presence of Jesus Christ" with the "explanatory models" used to account for it, especially the Catholic doctrine of transubstantiation and the Lutheran doctrine of ubiquity (I have modified the translations in light of the German original). Like its American predecessor, this dialogue also appeals to the ecumenical fruitfulness of the notion of "transignification"; cf. 99–100.

What Does It Mean to "Do This"?

This eclipse of interest in a theologically normative account of Christ's presence in the Eucharist has relegated one theological idea above all to the deep shadows: the Roman Catholic understanding of the real presence in terms of transubstantiation. This is often assumed, by Catholics at least as much as by Protestants and Orthodox, to be a needless rationalization of the mystery of Christ's eucharistic presence, implausibly based on an out-moded Greek metaphysics, and, as Luther argued at the beginning of the Reformation, an idea illicitly imposed upon the church by an overreaching Roman authority that ought simply to have encouraged faith in the truth of Christ's words, "This is my body."

In 1965, before the Second Vatican Council had yet concluded and a generation of ecumenical dialogue on the Eucharist begun, Pope Paul VI warned Catholics against the perils of ignoring what the Council of Trent had taught about transubstantiation and of supposing that Trent's formulas regarding the Eucharist are time-bound artifacts for which contemporary substitutes should be found, or upon which substantive improvements need to be made.[3] The "new wave of Eucharistic devotion" that Paul VI hoped would "sweep over the Church" as a result of the Council's "restoration of the sacred liturgy" depended, he argued, on a continued vigorous adherence to the doctrinal and pastoral teaching of the Council of Trent on the Eucharist.[4] This, it has to be said, belongs among those teachings of the Ordinary Papal Magisterium that have yet to be received in the church, perhaps especially by theologians. For the most part subsequent Catholic theology, including Catholic ecumenical dialogue, has completely ignored the admonitions of Paul VI and regarded traditional Catholic teaching on transubstantiation as at best one alternative among others for explaining the "how" of the Eucharist, should one wish to undertake that secondary and perhaps questionable project.[5]

3. See his Encyclical *Mysterium Fidei* (September 3, 1965), §§11, 24. The pope has in mind notions like "transignification" and "transfinalization," which Schillebeeckx and others had begun to employ as interpretations of Catholic teaching. While correct as far as they go, these cannot, Paul VI insists, be the basis of an adequate interpretation of Trent's eucharistic doctrine. See especially §46. I follow here the text of *Mysterium Fidei* on the Vatican Web site: http://www.vatican.va/holy_father/paul_vi/encyclicals/documents/hf_p-vi_enc_03091965_mysterium_en.html; the Latin typica of the encyclical may also be found there.

4. The quoted phrases are from *Mysterium Fidei* §§13 and 6.

5. At the time of its appearance *Mysterium Fidei* was greeted in some quarters with relief and gratitude. Asked by Paul VI to comment on a draft of the encyclical a month before it was issued, Charles Cardinal Journet offered the pope a number of comments,

It is surely legitimate and necessary to distinguish between the fact of Christ's Eucharist presence and how he is present. We can and should make a distinction, in other words, between affirming the fact of Christ's real presence in the Eucharist and conceiving the precise manner in which his body and blood are related to or connected with the consecrated bread and wine. Furthermore, we ought to distinguish between how Christ is present and the way in which his presence comes about. Thus, three distinct issues are basic to thinking about the real presence: *that* Christ is present, *how* he is present, and the way his presence *comes to be*. These three issues are closely intertwined, of course, but trying to keep them straight will be an aid to clarity in seeking to understand Christ's eucharistic presence.

Nevertheless it is a mistake, with potentially grave consequences, to play the fact off against the "how," or to suppose that there are no telling choices to be made between different ways of understanding how Christ is present, and comes to be present, for our salvation in the Eucharist. Paul VI was right, I think, to insist that not every way of understanding the real presence is equally correct, adequate, or helpful.

Like all the mysteries of the faith, the fact of Christ's real presence in the Eucharist elicits the believing mind's effort to understand it, and to grasp, insofar as the light available in this life allows, how it comes to be. To insist that we cling to the fact while suspending judgment on how the fact may rightly be understood is self-defeating. We can't help yearning for the light shed upon what we believe by having reasons that help us understand it. If we become convinced that we can't have these reasons, that there simply is no light by which the fact may be seen more clearly, eventually we are likely to give up believing in the fact itself. This is the mind's natural response, it would seem, to truth claims that come to it on good authority, but that it finds it can make no headway in understanding.

I will offer here a brief series of thoughts on how Christ's eucharistic presence might not only be believed in but also understood. As I hope will be easily apparent, I intend these thoughts to follow closely what I take to be the logic of established Catholic doctrine on Christ's true, real, and substantial presence in the Eucharist, and on transubstantiation as the

---

and said in his cover letter, "This is one of the great joys of my life. The agony which weighed on us has vanished. The faith of the Church is saved." *Journet Maritain Correspondance*, vol. 6, *1965–1973* (Éditions Saint-Augustin, 2008) 795. Journet was in the minority, and theological criticism of the encyclical set in soon after it was issued. A generation later, though, *Mysterium Fidei* would be cited to telling effect in the *Catechism of the Catholic Church*. See §§1374 and 1378.

"most apt" way to understand how this presence comes about.[6] But I will not develop these thoughts, except in passing, by way of an exegesis of the Council of Trent or other authoritative Catholic teaching on the Eucharist. My hope is thus to present what I take to be the binding doctrinal content of, and the theological reasons for, this central Catholic teaching in a way that will also make sense to non-Catholics who accept the real presence as a fact.

Christian Mystery and the Logic of Identity

To believe in the real presence is to accept the truth of two statements as spoken by Jesus, and by those whom he has authorized to say them in his stead.[7] The first statement is "This is my body," and the second, "This is the chalice of my blood." Both of these are identity statements. Or, more precisely, believing in the real presence requires recognizing that, as spoken by Jesus and those whom he has authorized, they are both identity statements.

We make an identity statement when we say that one thing is the same as another. "Sandra Marshall's husband is Nancy Marshall's firstborn son" is an identity statement. It asserts that the two descriptions, "Sandra Marshall's husband" and "Nancy Marshall's firstborn son," refer or apply to the same individual, namely me. "The evening star is the morning star" is an identity statement in just the same way, a philosophically famous test case for how to understand identity statements. Asserting the identity of one thing with another is among the irreducibly basic uses of the term "is."

Of course, not every use of the term "is" asserts identity. We often use "is" to attribute a property or characteristic to something, to say of this or that thing that it has a feature that also belongs, or could belong, to others. The statement "Sandra Marshall's husband is going bald" uses "is" in this attributive way. It doesn't assert that the descriptions "Sandra Marshall's husband" and "going bald" are co-extensive. Sandra Marshall's husband has other features besides going bald, and lots of people are going bald besides

---

6. In the phrase of canon 2 of Trent's Decree on the Eucharist, DH 1652 (DH = Heinrich Denzinger, *Enchiridion Symbolorum: A Compendium of Creeds, Definitions, and Declarations of the Catholic Church* (Latin-English), 43rd ed., ed. Peter Hünermann [San Francisco: Ignatius, 2012]). All translations are my own.

7. Who may be regarded as so authorized is, of course, a matter of significant disagreement among Christians. For present purposes we can leave this to one side, though it is a matter of deep ecumenical significance, and one on which the best efforts of ecumenists have so far made little progress.

Sandra Marshall's husband. Thus philosophers distinguish between the "is" of identity, used to assert that one thing is the same as another, and the "is" of predication, used to assert that an individual thing or a kind of thing has a given feature, but the thing or class and the feature are not the same.[8]

At the heart of Christian faith lies a sequence of three identity statements, or perhaps better, three families of identity statements linked in a certain order, and linked also to equally important denials of identity. These identity statements are at the heart of Christian faith in the mysteries of the Trinity, the incarnation, and the Eucharist, respectively.

> (1) "Jesus Christ [is] true God from true God." This creedal identity statement asserts that Jesus Christ is the same as God. It follows another creedal identity statement: "God [is] the Father almighty." This latter statement asserts that the one God is the same as the Father. By saying that Jesus Christ is "true God from true God," that is, God from the Father, the Creed further asserts that Jesus Christ is not the same as the Father. If he were identical with the Father, he would not be from him. The Creed thus makes two identity statements, and denies a third: "The Father is the same as the one God," and "Jesus Christ is the same as the one God," but "Jesus Christ is not the same as the Father." The Creed makes (or implies) a cognate series of identity statements about the Holy Spirit. The Spirit is "the Lord and giver of life," and so is the same as the one God, but the Spirit proceeds from the Father—or, in later Catholic teaching, from the Father and the Son—and so is not the same as either. To believe in the Holy Trinity is to hold true these assertions and denials of identity, as a great many Christians do explicitly in the liturgy each Sunday.[9]

Upon this first family of identity statements depends a second:

> (2) "Our Lord Jesus Christ . . . begotten of the Father from eternity, is the same as the one begotten of the Virgin Mary, the God-bearer, in these last days." This statement of the Council of Chalcedon asserts the identity, the sameness, of the Father's Son and Mary's Son, of the one born of the Father before all time with the one born of the Virgin Mary in time. The one who is "complete in divinity" on account of his eternal origination from the Father

8. This is not, to be sure, a full taxonomy of the uses of "is." We use the "is" of predication to sort or classify particulars into kinds, and not only to attribute characteristics to the particulars or kinds thus sorted; thus, "Socrates is a human being." Identity and characterization are, however, the two uses of "is" most pertinent to our present concern.

9. The quoted phrases are from the Creed of 381, DH 150.

is the same as the one who is "complete in humanity" on account of his origination in time from the Virgin Mary. But divinity is not the same as humanity. Rather the two are united in one and the same Lord Jesus Christ "without confusion, without change." To believe in the incarnation of the Son of God is to hold true these assertions and denials of identity.[10]

On this second family of identity statements depends a third:

(3) "This is my body," "This is my blood," said by Jesus and his authorized representatives of the bread and wine before them when they begin to speak. These statements assert the identity, the sameness, of what is on the altar when each utterance is complete with the body and blood of Jesus. They also imply a pair of denials. What is on the altar after these statements are made perceptibly retains the characteristics of bread and wine, and does not take on the perceptible characteristics of Jesus' body and blood. So what is on the altar, the host and what the chalice holds, are the as same Jesus' body and blood, but the characteristics of what is on the altar are not the characteristics of Jesus' body and blood. To believe in the real presence is, once again, to hold true these two assertions of identity, and the correlative denials they imply.

In Christian history each of these three sorts of identity statement—those necessary for faith in the Trinity, the incarnation, and the real presence, respectively—has been vehemently contested, and the truth of each denied, sometimes blatantly, sometimes more subtly. It is not hard to understand why. Unlike, for example, "Sandra Marshall's husband is Nancy Marshall's firstborn son," each of Christianity's core identity statements asserts what does not seem possible to the human mind untutored by divine teaching. We believe them to be true by relying in faith on the truthfulness of God who teaches them to us. As Thomas Aquinas's hymn "Adoro te devote" says of the real presence—the statement "This is my body," in particular—"I believe whatever the Son of God has said: there is nothing more true than this word of the one who is the Truth."[11]

Each of the identity statements at the heart of Christian faith poses its own deep problem for human understanding, not quite the same as that posed by the other two. In each case, though, if we would obtain some measure of understanding we need to make progress in saying how two things

10. The quoted phrases are from the Definition of Chalcedon, DH 301–2.

11. It sounds better, and the thought is clearer, in the original: *Credo, quidquid dixit Dei Filius: / Nil hoc verbo Veritatis verius.*

can be the same which don't seem to be the same, or whose identity with one another seems inconceivable. When it comes to "This is my body" and "This is my blood," the problem is especially obvious. How can a small piece of baked goods and a cup of fermented liquid be the same as the body and blood, indeed the total reality, of a human being? How can, for example, the whole body of a human being be present exactly where a tiny wafer is present, occupying precisely the space taken up by the little piece of bread?

Daunting as this sort of difficulty is, it is surely no more daunting than the difficulty posed by believing that the Father, the Son, and the Holy Spirit are not the same as each other, yet each is the same as the one God, or the difficulty posed by believing that the human being Jesus is the same as God the Son. Faith in the Trinity, the incarnation, and the real presence involves basically the same kind of claim in each case, and poses basically the same kind of difficulty. To disbelieve all three of these, for more or less the same sort of reason, would be understandable enough. It is much more difficult to understand how one could believe in the Trinity and the incarnation, and yet disbelieve in the real presence. Often enough Nicene Christians have contested the real presence on the grounds that the identity statements on which it is predicated make no sense—it is impossible to understand how what is on the altar could be the same as the body and blood of Jesus. But this seems inconsistent. The same kind of argument, easily adjusted to the different cases, could be made against the Trinity and the incarnation. These core Christian convictions come as a trio, and if a lack of understanding is a barrier to one, it is a barrier to all three. This underlines, of course, the importance of seeking an understanding of each.

Reasons for the Real Presence

It is striking to observe that Christians took "This is my body" and "This is my blood" to be genuine identity statements from the first, despite obvious cognitive difficulties posed by doing so. They insisted on it well before conceptual means began to be devised for understanding how these identity statements could be true.

Early in the second century, Ignatius of Antioch is already clear that the eucharistized bread and wine are the same as the body and blood of Christ. "The Eucharist," he writes to the church at Smyrna, "is the flesh of our savior Jesus Christ, that flesh which [not just 'who'] suffered for our sins but which the Father raised in his kindness."[12] Justin Martyr, in the earliest detailed description we have of the church's Eucharist (ca. 160), explains that as a result of the presider's prayer of thanksgiving, "the food which has been made Eucharist is both the flesh and the blood of that Jesus who was made flesh."[13]

This early unselfconscious insistence that the eucharistic food is the same as the one body and blood of Christ stems, no doubt, from already established apostolic tradition that this is how the Lord's words in the upper room are to be taken, whatever the evidence of the senses. As Cyril of Alexandria would later write, "When the Lord says, 'This is my body, which will be given up for you,' doubt not whether this is true, but rather receive the words of the savior in faith, for he does not lie."[14] Later still Thomas Aquinas follows this ancient tradition when he writes, citing this very text of Cyril, "That the true body and blood of Christ are in this sacrament cannot be grasped by the senses, but only by faith (*sola fide*), which relies upon the authority of God himself."[15] That the Eucharist is the same as Christ's body and blood, and thus that the words of Jesus solemnly uttered by the eucharistic celebrant are, at their completion, genuine identity statements, was evidently embraced as an irreducibly basic element of the apostolic faith from the earliest times.

Christians have, nonetheless, often questioned the correctness of this ancient consensus. Well before the Reformation, this led theologians to offer arguments as to why we should take (or continue to take) the words of Christ in the traditional way. Reflection on three such arguments will help to give a sense both of the depth at which the conviction holds that Christ's own body and blood are really present on the altar, and the precise difficulties this conviction offers to faith seeking understanding.

---

12. *To the Smyrnaeans* 7:1. That there is only one flesh of Christ, present in every Eucharist, is the basis, Ignatius insists, of the unity of the church: "So be diligent to use one Eucharist for there is [only] one flesh of our Lord Jesus Christ and one cup for unity in his blood. There is one altar as there is one bishop" (*To the Philadelphians* 4). The translations are those of Kenneth J. Howell, *Ignatius of Antioch: A New Translation and Theological Commentary* (Zanesville, OH: CH Resources, 2008) 113, 104. See also Howell's helpful essay in the same volume, "The Eucharist in the Theology of Ignatius," 47–52.

13. *1 Apology* 66. "Made" here clearly means "changed into" (*metabole*). On this more later.

14. *In Lucam* 22:19 (PG 72, 912A-B).

15. *Summa theologiae* III, 75, 1, c.

(1) One such reason lies in the shape of salvation history, particularly the way in which salvation through Christ is mediated to God's people before his coming in the flesh and after. The Old Testament already included sacraments which served as signs or figures of the grace of Christ, such as circumcision, the Passover lamb, and the myriad rituals of the Levitical cult, both within and without the temple. These "sacraments of the Old Law," as they were sometimes called, effectively pointed to the future, as signs sometimes do. They directed God's people to Christ's saving work yet to come, and by pointing effectively to the paschal mystery they mediated to Israel the saving grace of Christ in an anticipatory way (in scholastic terms, as final causes).

If the sacraments established by Christ himself did no more, if they too were only effective signs of his saving work, there would be no need for them. That Christ established new sacraments which would make present his saving work definitively until the end of time—especially the Eucharist, in which not only the saving power of the cross, but he himself, the crucified, is present in his total reality—is precisely the difference the cross makes when it actually comes to pass. The cross transforms the world, first and most importantly by transforming the means and the way in which the crucified makes himself present to the world. Differently put: "If salvation were through the law, then Christ died to no purpose" (Gal 2:21). This is one sort of reason, very common in the tradition, that Christians have had for taking "This is my body" as an identity statement.[16]

(2) Another reason is eucharistic sacrifice. That the Eucharist is a sacrifice, the sacrifice of Christians commanded by Christ, for fifteen centuries it would never have occurred to Christians to doubt, as the Anglican bishop and theologian Mark Santer observes.[17] One obvious reason for this is that Christ said "Do this," that is, do just what I have done, and what Christ did was offer his body and blood to the Father sacramentally for the salvation of the world, an offering made once for all in the upper room and consummated on the cross. Protestant hand-wringing about whether we can actually offer Christ to God in the Eucharist is hard to understand in light of the institution narratives. He *told* us to, so it must be possible to do it. He

---

16. For one version of this argument, see Aquinas, *Summa theologiae* III, 75, 1, c; for the tie to Gal 2:21, note the discussions in I–II, 103, 2; III, 62, 6; and III, 70, 1.

17. In his preface to Kenneth Stevenson, *Eucharist and Offering* (New York: Pueblo, 1986) vii.

offered himself once for all to the Father for the salvation of the world, and then told us to do just the same thing.

We cannot, however, offer Christ's body and blood to the Father if what we offer in the Eucharist isn't the same as Christ's body and blood. So the sacrificial character of the Eucharist is another reason for believing in the real presence. This can be put the other way around. Sacrifice is an act, so a sacrifice—here, of course, the sacrifice of Christ—can be present only as offered, more precisely, only insofar as an act of offering is present. And this is just what the words of institution require. "This is my body," Jesus says, "which will be given up for you." So if his body is really present in the Eucharist, it is not just his body abstractly considered, but his body sacrificed—sacrificed, of course, by himself. And if his blood is really present in the Eucharist, it is precisely his blood poured out, sacrificed, for the forgiveness of sins—sacrificed, again, by himself. It is this sacrifice that's made present again when Jesus' representative says "This is my body" over bread and "This is my blood" over wine. It is this sacrifice, his own, that Jesus bids us take into our own unworthy hands, offer to the Father, and receive on our tongues. He leaves us no room to plead our unworthiness against his simple command: do this.[18]

(3) A third reason for taking "This is my body" as a genuine identity statement has to do, we could say, with the purpose for which Christ gave the Eucharist to us, the end that moved him to establish it. He gives us this supreme gift out of love, in order that we might be his friends, and indeed to perfect the bond of friendship with us (cf. John 15:15). Aquinas offers this among the ways we can understand why Christ makes himself present truly, and not just figuratively, in the Eucharist—reasons why what Christ has in fact done and taught by his utterances in the upper room is "appropriate" or "suitable" (*conveniens*) to our condition.

> This fits with the charity of Christ, which moved him to assume a true body of our nature for our salvation. Because it is especially characteristic of friendship that "friends live together," as the philosopher says (*Ethics* IX), Christ promises us his bodily presence as our [final] reward. . . . Yet in the meantime he has not left us destitute of his bodily presence while we are on this pilgrimage,

18. For an excellent account of the bond between the real presence and eucharistic sacrifice, drawing on the profound eucharistic theology of Maurice de la Taille's *Mysterium Fidei*, see Michon M. Matthiesen, *Sacrifice as Gift: Eucharist, Grace, and Contemplative Prayer in Maurice de la Taille* (Washington, DC: Catholic University of America Press, 2013).

but joins us to himself in this sacrament by the truth of his body and blood. Thus he says, "He who eats my flesh and drinks my blood remains in me, and I in him" (John 6:57). Hence this sacrament, because it brings about such an intimate union of Christ to us, is a sign of the greatest charity, and consoles us with hope.[19]

The Eucharist is Christ's answer, prepared in advance, to the plea that marks the whole of our earthly journey: "Stay with us, Lord, for evening draws near, and the day is now far spent" (Luke 24:29).[20] It is his enactment for us of the love that never ends (1 Cor 13:8), the love that makes us forever his intimate friends. In the Eucharist Jesus unites our body to his, in the intimacy that only friends enjoy. And so we now enjoy, already on this earthly pilgrimage, the bond of friendship among embodied persons in which our final blessedness will consist. We may approach the Eucharist, therefore, in prayer for the consummation of the friendship this sacrament already creates. "Most loving Father, grant that in the end I may forever look upon your beloved Son face to face, whom on this earthly journey I now intend to receive under a veil."[21]

To be sure, our ultimate and beatifying union with Christ's body will be of a different kind than the union we now enjoy. Blessedness will depend on the vision of that body, rather than on hearing about it, and will as such be immeasurably more intense than our present union with his body and blood in Holy Communion. Nevertheless, Christ in his mercy and generosity offers us in this life a *kind* of union with him, bodily present, that we will not enjoy in the end: the eating and drinking of him, bodily present. While this present intimacy will give way to a yet greater one, as faith gives way to sight, the communion of his body and blood is nonetheless a greater intimacy than we could have with him if we were to see him *now*, under the conditions of this life. Even the apostles on the Emmaus road, who saw his risen flesh, Christ nonetheless offered the intimacy of the Eucharist at

19. *Summa theologiae* III, 75, 1, c.

20. I owe this point to Reinhard Hütter, "Transubstantiation Revisited: *Sacra Doctrina*, Dogma, and Metaphysics," in *Ressourcement Thomism: Sacred Doctrine, the Sacraments, and the Moral Life: Essays in Honor of Romanus Cessario, OP,* ed. Reinhard Hütter and Matthew Levering (Washington, DC: Catholic University of America Press, 2010) 21–79, here 72.

21. In the words of a prayer before Mass traditionally attributed to Thomas Aquinas, but probably not from his hand: "O amantissime Pater, concede mihi dilectum Filium tuum, quem nunc velatum in via suscipere propono, revelata tandem facie perpetuo contemplari." For the text see *S. Thomae Aquinatis Opera Theologica,* ed. R Spiazzi and M. Calcaterra (Turin/Rome: Marietti, 1954) 2:287b.

the end of their journey: "Stay with us Lord, for evening draws near." The Eucharist, it seems, offers us the most intimate friendship we can have with Christ short of final beatitude. As such this friendship forms a particularly strong argument for what the Council of Trent will later call the "true, real, and substantial" presence of Christ in the sacrament.

Our friendship with Christ depends first of all not on our eating and drinking, but upon the very fact of his eucharistic presence with us. The prior fact of his real presence is what enables us to enjoy the uniquely intimate communion with him that takes place in the subsequent eating and drinking. That Christ offers his body to us in friendship by his very presence in the consecrated elements naturally unfolds into the continuation of this friendship outside the confines of the eucharistic rite itself. The real presence, in other words, naturally gives rise to what Catholics call the adoration of the Eucharist outside of Mass, or more precisely, the continued adoration of Christ, present in the Blessed Sacrament. This idea has ancient roots. Thus Augustine: Christ "took earth from the earth, for flesh is from the earth, and he received his flesh from the flesh of Mary. He walked here below in that very flesh, and even gave us that same flesh to eat for our salvation. But no one eats this flesh unless he has first adored it. . . . [N]ot only do we not sin in adoring it; we would sin if we did not adore it."[22]

The Semantics of the Eucharist

Christians thus have compelling reasons, linked to other convictions they regard as basic, for taking "This is my body" and "This is my blood" to be identity statements. This is also, I think, the natural way to take the words, and was clearly recognized as such from the early church to the end of the Middle Ages. The controversies that arose over this in the ninth century and again in the eleventh served to reinforce, rather than to weaken, the sense of Christians that this is what the words mean—that they assert the sameness of the elements they have consecrated with the body and blood of Christ.

In fact this would have to be the natural way to take the words, their plain or literal sense. Otherwise Christians from the beginning, and for centuries, would have taken them differently. Competent speakers of a language, after all, naturally and unselfconsciously take statements in their

22. *Expositions of the Psalms* 98.9, trans. Maria Boulding, ed. John Rotelle, The Works of St. Augustine III/18 (Hyde Park, NY: New City, 2002) 474–75 (translation altered).

language literally, and depart from the literal sense only when the context demands it. Not until the high Middle Ages did Christian theologians have available sophisticated semantic theories that might have provided a motive, independent of their natural sense, for interpreting the eucharistic words differently than had long been done.[23] In order briefly to see why it's natural, and not forced, to take "This is my body" as an identity statement, it will be helpful to recall the distinction between the "is" of identity and the "is" of predication.

How do we tell, when it comes to cases, whether to take two terms joined by "is" as identified, or not? We can't simply choose to take each case as seems best to us. It depends, rather, on what sort of terms are joined in the statement. Recall the example: we take "Sandra Marshall's husband is Nancy Marshall's firstborn son" as an identity statement, a case of the "is" of identity, because the statement joins one particular to another. The subject of the sentence is a term referring to a particular, which is standard, but the predicate is a different term that also refers to a particular. When we say one particular or individual "is" another, we can only be saying that in fact they are not two particular things, but one and the same particular thing, though described differently by the subject and by the predicate. The statement is true just in case the particular thing referred to by the subject and that referred to by the predicate are in fact one and the same, and false if they are not. Either way, though, we can tell whether we are dealing with an identity statement by seeing whether one particular is predicated of another.

Going bald, by contrast, is not a particular, but a characteristic possessed by some particulars and not by others. When we attribute to a person a term referring to this characteristic, we are precisely not saying that what's referred to by the subject of the sentence is one and the same as the characteristic referred to by the predicate. We're saying that this subject has this characteristic, and our sentence is true just in case he does, and false if he doesn't. The proposition "Sandra Marshall's husband is going bald" doesn't say that being Sandra Marshall's husband and going bald are one and the same thing, but that this particular and this characteristic are two distinct things, which could exist apart from one another, though as it happens they don't. We can tell when we have a case of the "is" of predication,

23. This in fact seems to have been a good part of what led Berengar, in the eleventh century, to question the identity of what is on the altar with the body of Christ. On the significant role of semantic theory in medieval eucharistic theology, see Irène Rosier-Catach, *La parole efficace: Signe, ritual, sacré* (Paris: Éditions du Seuil, 2004).

as opposed to the "is" of identity, when "is" joins not two particulars, but a particular, which can exist on its own, and a property or characteristic, which cannot, but must belong to some particular.

Seen in this light, to take the words of Jesus repeated in each Eucharist as an identity statement is to take them in their natural or plain sense. The demonstrative "this," referring to what is on the table before him, and "my body," are both terms referring to particulars. The copula "is," therefore, identifies them.

Now consider the following case: "This is a sign of my body." Being a sign of someone's body looks like a characteristic something has, in the manner of going bald, and not like a particular, in the manner of some bread or a cup. When "this" refers to the bread and cup of the Eucharist, then, it seems natural to take "This is a sign of my body" as a case of the "is" of predication, in which the characteristic of being a sign of Jesus' body is attributed to the bread and cup on the altar or table. Interpreted in its natural sense this statement thus differs fundamentally from the statement Jesus makes at the Last Supper, since Jesus makes an identity statement, and "This is a sign of my body" is not that kind of statement. The two statements are not interchangeable; they do not say the same thing, and one cannot be taken as an interpretation or explanation of the other.

Furthermore, being a sign of someone's body, unlike going bald, is a relational characteristic. When correctly asserted it links in a particular way two distinct things. Signs are normally quite distinct from what they signify: stop signs from the law requiring the driver to stop, words from the things to which they refer, and so forth. By attributing to the bread and cup before the assembly the characteristic of being a sign of Jesus' body and blood, which remain quite distinct from them, the statement "This is a sign of my body" seems doubly forced and unnatural as an interpretation of Jesus' words at the Last Supper. Both the form of the statement and the content of the predicate belie the identity statement made by Jesus.

All of this was long intuitively obvious in the tradition, and it was often made explicit. In a particularly direct passage, Theodore of Mopsuestia writes (expressing, as Paul VI observes, the faith of the church on this matter), "[The Lord] did not say: 'This is a symbol of my body, and this is a symbol of my blood,' but, 'This is my body and my blood.' He teaches us not to look at the nature of what lies before us, for the giving of thanks over it have changed it into flesh and blood."[24] That Christ is not present in the

24. *In Matthaeum fragmenta* (on Matt 26:26); PG 66, 713B. Cited (from the Latin

Eucharist only in the manner in which the symbolized is in the symbol, or the thing signified in the sign, is a commonplace of belief in the real presence from the ancient church on.[25]

By this point I'm sure the objection will already have come to mind that the Fathers do often speak of the Eucharist as a sign or "figure," as do the Western doctors after them. In fact Thomas Aquinas, among others, argues that the sacraments belong first of all in "the genus of signs," although they are signs of a distinctive sort, namely those which effect or bring about what they signify.[26] The statement, "This is a sign of my body," referring to the bread and cup of the Eucharist, cannot therefore simply be false.

Exactly so, and I think the foregoing reflections on different kinds of statements help us understand the sense in which the Eucharist is a sign or symbol. Especially in the West from the Middle Ages on, the Eucharist has been seen to have a twofold signification or sign value. The consecrated bread and wine (or more precisely their species, evident to the senses) are material signs of the body and blood of Christ, and the body and blood of Christ are themselves signs of the unity of the church, of incorporation into Christ's one mystical body, which the communion of his body and blood effects. Our present concern is with the first of these.

That the consecrated bread and wine of the Eucharist are genuine signs is indispensable to our apprehension of the real presence. Seen with faith in the truth of Christ's words we have heard spoken in the Eucharist, they are the needed means by which we creatures of sense are able to know precisely where Christ is really present, and thereby are also able to know that he is really present. His whole body, and all that belongs to his body, are present just where the material sign of consecrated bread is present, and his blood, and all that belongs to his blood, are present just where the material sign of the consecrated cup of wine is present. To say this, however, is already to suggest that these are signs unique in all creation. For unlike any others, these signs fully contain the reality they signify. The body and blood of Christ are not to be sought apart from these signs, but in them. In his

version) in *Mysterium Fidei*, §44.

25. Thus, e.g., Aquinas, *Summa theologiae* III, 75, 1, c: "Certain [theologians] proposed . . . that the body and blood of Christ are in this sacrament only as in a sign. This is to be rejected as heretical, since it is contrary to the words of Christ." Aquinas refers to Berengar in particular.

26. III, 73, 2, ob 2: "sign is the genus of a sacrament"; cf. 60, 1 for a fuller statement of the point.

total reality—body, blood, soul, and divinity, as Catholics like to say—Jesus Christ is just where they are.[27]

Another look at the statement "This is a sign of my body" may help here. The predicate "a sign of" is most readily taken to designate a characteristic or property. But a sign can also be taken simply as a thing, a particular. Read in that way, "This is a sign of my body" now makes sense as an identity statement: the bread is the same as a sign; the cup of wine is the same as a sign. And that, as we have just seen, is clearly true—as long as we take the predicates "sign of my body," "sign of my blood" in the otherwise unexampled sense of a sign used by what is signified to make itself wholly present exactly where the sign is.

Presence, Substance, and Conversion

I have already pointed out two patristic passages, one from Justin Martyr and one from Theodore of Mopsuestia, which tie belief in the real presence of Christ in the Eucharist to a radical change that takes place in the elements of bread and wine. Both say that this change is brought about by the words spoken at the Eucharist over the elements. Many further patristic texts could be cited to this effect—Ambrose in particular comes to mind—to say nothing of later writers.[28] I'll conclude with some thoughts about eucharistic conversion and its relationship to Christ's real presence in the Eucharist. At just at this point, I think, we've reached the heart of the matter.

The reality of this utterly singular change is surely the core doctrinal content of the much-contested Catholic teaching on transubstantiation. What is presented at the offertory is mere bread and wine, but by the power of Christ's words on the lips of his minister, they are changed into something quite different, his own body and blood. In Trent's words: "By

27. For Aquinas's way of putting the first point—that the eucharistized elements are signs of Christ's body and blood (the *sacramentum tantum* of the Eucharist, in his technical terminology)—see III, 73, 6, c and especially 80, 4, c. On the Eucharist as fully containing the reality it signifies, see III, 73, 1, ad 3; 73, 5, ad 2; 78, 1, c.

28. E.g., Ambrose, *The Mysteries*, 9.52: "Cannot the words of Christ, which were able to make what was not out of nothing, change those things that are into the things that were not?"; *The Sacraments* IV.iv.19: "From bread the body of Christ is made. And what is wine, water? It is put in the cup, but it becomes blood by heavenly consecration." *Saint Ambrose: Theological and Dogmatic Works*, trans. Roy J. Deferrari (Washington, DC: Catholic University of America Press, 1963) 25, 304.

the consecration of bread and wine there takes place the conversion of the whole substance of the bread into the substance of the body of Christ our Lord, and of the whole substance of the wine into his blood. It is this conversion," the Council adds, "that is suitably and rightly called transubstantiation by the Holy Catholic Church."[29] As the wording of both this passage and the coordinated canon 2 makes clear, "conversion," the change of one thing into another, is the basic concept here. "Transubstantiation" is another "suitable" term for this conversion, naturally so, since both the thing changed and that into which it is changed are substances (on which more momentarily). In Trent's teaching on the Eucharist, "conversion" thus explains the meaning of "transubstantiation," rather than the other way around.[30]

If this conversion is the normative content of the Catholic doctrine of transubstantiation, then as the philosopher Elizabeth Anscombe observes, any five year old who is reasonably attentive at Mass can get the point of

---

29. Decree on the Eucharist, ch. 4 (DH 1642). Canon 2 puts the point of the last clause a bit more strongly: the church "most aptly" (*aptissime*) calls the eucharistic conversion "transubstantiation" (DH 1652; cf. above, n. 6).

30. The theological debates at Trent that led up to the canons and decree on the Eucharist at Session XIII underline this point. In an influential *votum* (expert opinion) of February 1547, while the Council was meeting in Bologna, the Franciscan theologian Johannes Consilii replied to Calvin's repudiation of the term "transubstantiation" as a medieval scholastic novelty. He observed that this word added nothing to what was already meant by the terms common among various church fathers, such as "mutatio," "conversio," and "transformatio." "While the word is more recent, the faith and the thing are nonetheless most ancient" (*Concilium Tridentinum . . . nova collectio* [Freiburg: Herder, 1901–], vol. 5, 945.50).

When the Council resumed back in Trent in the fall of 1551, after a hiatus of four years, the Dominican theologian Melchior Cano made the same point in a still more forceful way. While it employs the term "transsubstantiatio," the Fourth Lateran Council (1215) should not be read, Cano argues, as though it made the term itself essential to Catholic faith in the Eucharist. Lateran IV "mentions transubstantiation, but this does not appear to belong to the faith." In this matter the heretic is not the person who doubts the usefulness of this relatively recent term, "but the one who asserts that the bread is not converted into the body of Christ" (*Concilium Tridentinum*, vol. 7/1, 125.9–13). The final formulation of Trent's canon 2 on the Eucharist follows Cano closely on this point, as Hubert Jedin observes in his detailed analysis of the theological discussions at the Council (*Geschichte des Konzils von Trient*, vol. 3, *Bologneser Tagung (1547/48)—Zweite Trienter Tagunsperiode (1551/52)* [Freiburg: Herder, 1970] 271). Jedin also shows (48) that the Council clearly meant to maintain a distinction, evident inter alia in the *vota* of Consilii and Cano, between the doctrinal truths it was teaching and the language in which they were taught.

the doctrine, though it seems to elude many theologians.[31] A wondrous event has taken place in our midst, a stupendous act of divine power that exceeds even creation *ex nihilo* in its unfathomable reach. At a precise point in time, and by ordinary human words, what was bread and wine has become something totally different. It is no longer bread and wine—though it still looks like those ordinary objects—it is Christ's body and his blood. It is Jesus himself, whole and entire, present to us in a manner far more wonderful, in fact, than if we could see him with our eyes and touch him with our hands, a manner, as Trent says, that words can scarcely begin to express.[32] He is present to us in this way out of love, so that we may do what we could never do if our eyes could see him and our hands could touch him: eat him, and live because of him (John 6:57).[33] He is present in this way so that we can be joined to him far more intimately than sight and touch would allow, as our very food, that food which truly gives life because it turns us into what it is, rather than being turned by us into what we are. Unlike bodily food, Aquinas comments (following a long tradition), "spiritual food is not transformed into the one who eats it, but transforms him into itself. Hence the proper effect of this sacrament is the transformation of the human being into Christ, so that he may say with the Apostle, 'It is no longer I who live, but Christ who lives in me' (Gal 2:20)."[34]

---

31. G. E. M. Anscombe, "On Transubstantiation" (1974), in *Faith in a Hard Ground: Essays on Religion, Philosophy and Ethics*, ed. Mary Geach and Luke Gormally (Exeter, UK: Imprint Academic, 2008) 84–91. Anscombe tells of a three-year-old whom she heard ask his mother, as she returned from communion, "Is he in you?" "Yes," the mother replied, "and to her amazement the child prostrated itself before her." Anscombe comments: "I once told the story to one of those theologians who unhappily (as it seems) strive to alter and to water down our faith, and he deplored it: he wished to say, and hoped the Vatican Council would say, something that would show the child's idea to be wrong. I guessed that the poor wretch was losing the faith and indeed so, sadly, did it turn out" (ibid., 86).

32. "Our Savior himself . . . is sacramentally present to us in his own substance, in a manner of existing which, although we can scarcely express it in words, is nevertheless possible for God." Decree on the Eucharist, ch. 1 (DH 1636).

33. Thus Trent's Decree on the Eucharist, ch. 2: "Our Savior . . . willed that this sacrament be consumed as the spiritual food of souls, by which they are nourished and strengthened, living by the life of the one who said, 'He who eats me will live because of me'" (DH 1638).

34. *In IV Sent.* d. 12, q. 2, a. 1, qla. i, sol. (= *Scriptum super Sententiis*, vol. 4, ed. M. F. Moos [Paris: Lethielleux, 1947] 524, §§165–66); cf. *Summa theologiae* III, 73, 3, ad 2, and Augustine, *Confessions* VII.x.16: "nec tu me in te mutabis sicut cibum carnis tuae, sed tu mutaberis in me."

As I suggested at the outset, three distinct claims are in play here: one concerning the fact of Christ's eucharistic presence, one concerning the "how" of Christ's presence, and one concerning the "way" in which that presence comes to be. Catholic teaching, in other words, affirms (1) that Christ is "truly, really, and substantially" present after the consecration (the fact); (2) that "the whole and complete Christ" is "contained" in the Eucharist "under the species of sensible things," so that "our Savior himself . . . is sacramentally present to us in his own substance" (the "how"); and (3) that "by the consecration of the bread and wine there takes place the conversion of the whole substance of the bread into the substance of the body of Christ our Lord, and of the whole substance of the wine into the substance of his blood." (the "way" the presence comes to be).[35]

In Catholic eucharistic doctrine the term "substance" figures in the articulation of all three claims. Perhaps for this reason the whole package of teaching is sometimes called "the Catholic doctrine of transubstantiation," although properly speaking transubstantiation concerns only the last of the three, the conversion of bread and wine into Christ's body and blood. In modern eucharistic theology not only the long-disputed term "transubstantiation," but the more basic term "substance," has often come to seem at best unfortunate in this context, prompting Catholic theologians in particular to search for happier substitutes. This effort, as we saw, has met with considerable resistance from the Catholic Magisterium.

The basic worry about "substance" seems to be twofold. The term belongs in the realm of metaphysics, and its use loads Catholic eucharistic doctrine with philosophical technicalities precisely at a point of unsurpassable practical and pastoral significance. Still worse, the "substantialist" metaphysics with which Trent's language burdens Catholic doctrine is at best markedly problematic, if not simply flawed and outmoded beyond recovery.

Rumors of the death of "substance metaphysics" are, I think, exaggerated. Recognizably Aristotelian metaphysical accounts of substances and their qualities continue to find sophisticated defenders, not least among analytic philosophers. But in any case Trent's chapters and canons on the

---

35. The quoted phrases from Trent's decree and canons on the Eucharist are in (1) ch. 1 (DH 1636) and canon 1 (DH 1651); (2) ch. 3 (DH 1641), ch. 1 (DH 1636) and canon 1 (DH 1651); (3) ch. 4 (DH 1642) and canon 2 (DH 1652). More broadly speaking, we can say that ch. 1 deals with the fact of Christ's presence, ch. 3 with its precise manner, and ch. 4 with the way it comes about. Ch. 2 concerns the reasons Christ instituted the Eucharist; we have touched on this above.

Eucharist do not use the term "substance" in a technical way, nor do they mandate, or even invoke, any particular metaphysical construal of the concept of substance. The same goes, *a fortiori*, for their use of the derivative term "transubstantiation."

This interpretation of Trent's teaching on the Eucharist is not a contemporary gloss (prompted, one might suppose, by typically modern metaphysical squeamishness), but was clearly evident at the Council itself. Making a point often reiterated at Trent, one Benedictine abbot urged the Council Fathers to "remember that we are here to make laws not for the learned and expert, but for uneducated people, who are beset by so many liars and opponents." This required the clearest possible demarcation of Catholic teaching from newly-arisen heresies, but it did not require the resolution of school differences among theologians. In fact it was frequently urged at Trent, from Cardinal-Presidents on down, that the Council's business was to condemn heresy, not to settle theological, let alone philosophical, debates within the Catholic fold. As the same Benedictine abbot observed, questions should be settled in such a way that "we do not excite disturbances in the schools and sow causes of dissension among scholars."[36]

The Council of Trent evidently uses the term "substance" not in a way you have to have mastered Aristotle's *Metaphysics* to understand, but in a simple and basic sense, what could be called an ordinary language meaning of the term. "Substance" is what a thing is. Or a bit more precisely, substance is a thing of a definite kind that exists independently, or on its own. Catholic teaching holds that Christ is not only "truly and really," but "substantially," present in the Eucharist, and that he is present "in his own substance." This means that Christ himself is what the (consecrated) thing on the altar is, and that he is present on the altar in his own reality—as the sort of thing that exists independently—and not as a part or feature of something else. Catholic teaching also holds that the eucharistic consecration changes one whole substance into another, this bread and this wine into Christ's body and blood (the doctrine of transubstantiation strictly speaking). It thereby claims, radically but quite simply, that a thing of one kind is entirely changed into a thing of another kind. By the power of Christ's own words, what was one thing, existing on its own, has become another, quite different, thing, existing on its own. To deny *this* is not to

36. The quotations are from *Concilium Tridentinum*, vol. 6/2, 11.32–33, 40–41; the speaker was Chrysostom, abbot of the monastery of the Holy Trinity in Gaeta. For the deployment in the eucharistic debates of the principle that the Council would not settle scholastic disputes, see Jedin, *Geschichte des Konzils von Trient*, 3:51, 273–74, 282.

eschew a needless and misleading metaphysical technicality, but to deny the eucharistic conversion itself.

One may surely ask, though, what's wrong with denying the eucharistic conversion. Why should belief in the real (and for that matter, substantial) presence of Christ in the Eucharist require belief in the change of one substance into another in the first place? Catholic doctrine, of course, presents substantial conversion as an integral part of the church's faith in the Eucharist, and holds the denial of this conversion to be a grave error. Many Protestants, however, say that they believe in the real presence just as Catholics do, but see no need to tie their faith in the real presence to a teaching on substantial conversion. It would be a fruitful and legitimate ecumenical step, so Protestants therefore suggest, for the Catholic Church to acknowledge a shared faith in the real presence with many Protestants, and to leave transubstantiation as the distinctively Catholic way—but not the only way—of understanding how this presence comes about.

In fact my own way of presenting the faith of Christians in Christ's eucharistic presence, one might argue, actually betrays an inconsistency (perhaps a typically Catholic inconsistency) on this point. Constitutive of eucharistic faith, I claimed, is a pair of identity statements: "This is my body"; "This is the chalice of my blood." If these are genuine identity statements as I proposed, then what they must mean is "This *bread* is my body" and "This *wine* is my blood." By reverting to the Catholic doctrine of transubstantiation, where bread and wine alike are no longer present but have been wholly transformed into something else, I have actually shrunk from the implications of my own argument about the content of eucharistic faith. By Marshall's own lights, so the objection goes, something like "consubstantiation" (or "impanation," as it was called in the Middle Ages) does better justice to faith in the real presence than the traditional Catholic doctrine he is determined to defend.

Understood as this objection proposes, "This is my body" isn't an identity statement, but a contradiction in terms. It asserts, that is, an identity that cannot possibly obtain. In order for any two things we think of as distinct to be in fact one and the same—including bread and Christ's body—they have to have all the same properties or characteristics. But bread has many characteristics Christ's body lacks, and conversely. Bread, for example, is made of ground wheat and water, Christ's body of flesh and bone. As theological commentators on the real presence have observed since ancient times, it is no accident that Jesus, in instituting the Eucharist for us, said "This is my body," not "This bread is my body." For it is not a mystery, but a contradiction, to say that one and the same thing has the property of being made of ground wheat, and has the property of being made of flesh and bone—that is, not of ground wheat.[37]

Faith in Christ's eucharistic presence requires a denial of identity as well as an assertion of one. What is on the altar is identical with the body and blood of Christ, but Christ's body and blood have not thereby become bread and wine, or taken on the characteristics of bread and wine. This is the eucharistic counterpart to our denial, in the doctrine of the Trinity, that the Son is identical with the Father, and to our denial, in the doctrine of the incarnation, that humanity is identical with divinity. That the Father is one person and the Son another, yet they are one and the same God, is a mystery. That the human being Jesus has fallen a prey to death, and God the eternal Son is immortal, yet God the Son and the human being Jesus are one and the same person, is likewise a mystery. That mortality is immortality, or that the Son is his own Father, is not a mystery, but an absurdity. So also the claim that this bread is the same as Christ's body.

As a strategy for believing in the real presence without embracing the doctrine of transubstantiation the notion of impanation or consubstantiation so far seems unpromising. But the idea might be taken in a different way. One might hold that Christ's body is exactly where the consecrated bread is, though bread and body are not one and the same thing, and that Christ's blood is exactly where the consecrated wine are, though wine and blood are not the same thing. Rather the substance of Christ's body is contained under the substance of the bread, and his blood under the substance of the wine, in a manner not unlike that in which Catholic doctrine sees Christ's body and blood to be contained under the species or accidents of bread and wine. Nothing happens to the bread and wine as such; they are not transformed or converted into something else. Yet what is on the altar is radically different from what is was before the consecration. It is now true to say "This is Christ's body," though not, of course, "This bread is Christ's body."

What might a Catholic make of this way of understanding Christ's real presence in the Eucharist? It is striking to observe that John Duns Scotus and William of Ockham, two of the most influential theologians of the later

37. The English Dominican theologian Herbert McCabe rightly observes that "not even God could deem something both to be and not be bread and wine—except in different senses." "Eucharistic Change," in Herbert McCabe, *God Still Matters*, ed. Brian Davies (London: Continuum, 2002) 117.

Middle Ages, both hold that a position like that just described is a coherent and plausible alternative to transubstantiation. It would be possible for the real, substantial presence of Christ in the Eucharist, the presence in which Catholics believe on the basis of Christ's own words, to come about in this way. Or more precisely it would have *been* possible for Christ's substantial presence in the Eucharist to come about by impanation rather than by substantial conversion, had God so willed. Scotus and Ockham alike are emphatic that God has in fact willed to bring about Christ's eucharistic presence by substantial conversion, and not in any other way. In this they are at one with virtually all scholastic theologians from the mid-thirteenth century on, not least in view of Lateran IV's authoritative use of the language of transubstantiation.[38]

It is sometimes supposed, erroneously, that in arguing for the possibility of the real presence without substantial conversion Scotus, Ockham, and their many followers hold that the real presence actually comes about by impanation, or at least that it would be better to think of the real presence in such terms than to invoke substantial conversion. Were that the case, Trent's later insistence on transubstantiation could be seen as, in effect, the *post factum* condemnation of a large swath of medieval eucharistic theology. As Scotus and Ockham actually see it, however, Lateran IV has already established that transubstantiation is *de fide*, and both offer elaborate, though quite different, accounts of how to understand this essential Catholic teaching and defend it against objections.[39]

What's at stake in their defense of alternative possibilities is a bit more subtle. If transubstantiation is the only possible way for the real, substantial presence of Christ in the Eucharist to come about (as Thomas Aquinas, for example, influentially holds), then to reject transubstantiation is to reject the real presence as such.[40] To say that you believe in the real presence but

38. DH 802: "[T]he body and blood of [Jesus Christ himself] are truly contained under the species of bread and wine in the sacrament of the altar, the bread having been transubstantiated into his body, and the wine into his blood, by divine power."

39. Both Scotus and Ockham appeal to the text of Lateran IV cited in the previous note as establishing that Christ's eucharistic presence comes about by transubstantiation, though it is only one witness in a dossier of patristic and medieval authorities that decide the issue. See Scotus, *Ordinatio* IV, d. 11, p. 1, a. 2, q. 1, no. 135 (Vat. ed., vol. 12, 219); Ockham, *Tractatus de corpore Christi*, c. 4, in *Guillelmi de Ockham Opera Theologica*, vol. 10, ed. Charles A. Grassi (St. Bonaventure, NY: St. Bonaventure University Press, 1986) 96. The content of this dossier of authorities was largely established for scholastic authors from the thirteenth century on by Peter Lombard in Bk. 4 of his *Sentences*, dist. 10–11.

40. See, e.g., *Summa theologiae* III, 75, 4, c: "It is necessary to say that [the body of

not in transubstantiation is simply inconsistent. If you understood what you were saying, you would recognize that you had to choose between accepting transubstantiation and rejecting the real presence. But if, as Scotus and Ockham hold, transubstantiation is not the only way the real, substantial presence of Christ in the Eucharist could conceivably come about, then to reject transubstantiation is to be mistaken about a matter of grave importance. But it is not to reject the real presence as such. Those who believe in the real presence yet deny that a substantial conversion takes place in the Eucharist are wrong, but they are not inconsistent.

Trent's teaching on transubstantiation does not touch *this* question at all. It requires one to believe that the real presence actually comes about by transubstantiation, but it does not require one to believe that this is the only possible way the real presence could come about. This is precisely the sort of argument between opposing schools of Catholic theologians that the Council repeatedly disavows any intention of settling.[41] Over time the real presence and transubstantiation generally came to be seen, by Protestants and Catholics alike, as a package that has to be accepted or rejected as a whole (historic Lutheran teaching is the obvious exception to this generalization). The tendency of both sides to highlight their differences no doubt encouraged this perception. But seen against its broader medieval background Trent seems to leave open a modest but genuine ecumenical possibility on the real presence.

Normative Catholic doctrine on the Eucharist, as laid down at the Council of Trent, seemingly allows Catholics to hold that Christians who reject the doctrine of transubstantiation may nonetheless genuinely, and without inconsistency, believe in the real presence. To suppose that the presence of Christ's body and blood in the Eucharist comes about in some other way than by substantial conversion, or in some way unknown to us, is mistaken, and the mistake is not trivial. Nonetheless, Catholics need not take Protestant doubts about transubstantiation as tantamount to a denial of the real presence. If so, the way is open for Catholics to regard Protestant convictions about the real presence as not only sincere but, as far as they go, true. Thus Cardinal Ratzinger, as he then was, could argue that ecumenically, "the question of the Eucharist cannot be restricted to the

Christ] begins to be there by the conversion of the substance of the bread into itself"; cf. 75, 2.

41. In fact, so far as my own admittedly incomplete study of the *acta* has been able to discern, this question was never even discussed at Trent, let alone settled.

problem of 'validity.' Even a theology oriented to the concept of succession, as the Catholic and Orthodox Church maintains, must in no way deny a salvation-creating presence of the Lord in the Protestant Lord's Supper."[42]

At the same time, the ecumenical train presumably runs in both directions. It may be possible (that is, consistent and coherent) to believe in the real presence without believing in substantial conversion, the radical change of one thing into another. But *ought* one to do so? This is a question which, perhaps understandably, the ecumenical consensus of the last several generations has preferred not to ask. Yet if the days are largely past when Protestantism thought that, unable to believe in this change, it could not believe in the real presence, perhaps this question once again calls for an answer.

Rather than taking as basic our historic disagreement over transubstantiation, we might, as we think about this question, take as our point of departure the shared affirmation of the real presence of Christ in the Eucharist brought to light by the ecumenical dialogues of the last half-century. Our faith in the real presence might encourage us to look anew at the ancient idea of the conversion of the elements, so long seen by Christians as profoundly bound up with their confidence in the reality of Christ's gift of himself in the Eucharist. Does not our trust in Jesus' promise to be present when we obey his command, "Do this," urge us to embrace nothing less than the radical change of one substance into another, of mere bread and wine into the true body and blood of the one who made this promise, and gave this command?

---

42. Joseph Cardinal Ratzinger, *Pilgrim Fellowship of Faith: The Church as Communion*, ed. Stephen Otto Horn and Vinzenz Pfnür, trans. Henry Taylor (San Francisco: Ignatius, 2005) 248. I have modified the translation, especially the last clause, in light of the German original in *Una Sancta* (Meitingen) 48 (1993), a series of answers Cardinal Ratzinger gave to questions posed to him by the Lutheran bishop of Bavaria, Johannes Hanselmann: "Auch eine am Sukzessionsbegriff orientierte Theologie . . . muß keineswegs Heil schaffende Gegenwart des Herrn im evangelischen Abendmahl leugnen" (348).

4

What Do We Do with This? Ecumenical Implications of the Handling of the Eucharist

Peter Bouteneff

REFLECTING UPON CHRIST'S INJUNCTION to "do this in remembrance of me" (Luke 22:19) is a good way to frame the important and sensitive topic before us, an invitation to explore what the churches actually believe is happening at their celebration of the Supper. I was asked to address questions of "hospitality and intercommunion," and with this, presumably, the question of why some churches do not practice intercommunion.

My double task in this essay is suggested by my title: "What do we do with this?" For one, having digested the other contributions to this conference I have an opportunity to account for our discussions and say, "Now what do we do?" But "what do we do with this" also seeks to explore what we actually do with the elements of the Eucharist, the stuff that we gather to partake of. Because what we do with the bread and the wine (if that is what is being used) can often give more insight into our deepest sense of the Eucharist than a rehearsal of the technical debates about "real presence."

My program is as follows:

1. I will set out in rudimentary form the chief rationale, as I see it, for why my church does not practice open communion.

2. Among these reasons I will dwell briefly on the problem that we conceive of the Lord's Supper differently, and that terminology is just one symptom of this divergence.

3. To demonstrate convergences and differences, I will describe the practices for handling the eucharistic elements in four different church traditions and draw implications for how different churches conceive of the eucharist.

And so I begin by exploring some of the rationale for not sharing the Eucharist among churches that are—as is aptly put—not in communion. As something of an ecumenical veteran I have become accustomed to being the Orthodox representative who has to give the bad news about why we are separate and have to remain so for the time being. I have given papers at beautiful places that represent integration and union,[1] where I felt that people either expected me to fulfill that negative role or perhaps hoped that I would go against the stubborn culture of my church and advocate intercommunion because it is the loving and open thing to do. Such expectations have to be carefully reoriented, and it is not easy. I am grateful for your patience as I try.

1. Sharing the Eucharist

Any explanation for the Orthodox Church's restricted administration of the Eucharist would have to account for at least the following elements. I realize that some of these points are shared among several of the Christian confessions, others not.

a) It is impossible to talk about the Eucharist, and our inability to share it, without raising deep feelings of perplexity and hurt. The Eucharist is an intimate and powerfully felt thing. A church like mine, which does not offer the cup to those outside it and which forbids its members from communing outside it, can do its best to emphasize that this is not as such an act of exclusion. We can explain that it is a recognition of the nature of the sacrament, and of a thorough application of our

---

1. "Koinonia et communion eucharistique: Un point de vue Orthodoxe," *Irénikon* 73 (2000), translated in English as "Koinonia and Eucharistic Unity: An Orthodox Response," *The Ecumenical Review* 52 (2000) 72–80.

ecclesiology. But however one expresses it, painful feelings of exclusion inevitably remain. You may not believe it, and we don't always act like it, but the pain of not being in communion cuts both ways.

But pain is not always a terrible or inappropriate thing to feel. Let us be real with each other, and let us feel the pain. If we admit everyone to everyone's table simply because we abhor any and all exclusion, any pain, we are not being serious about our genuine differences over what the church is and what the Eucharist is. The Lord's Supper is not a catechetical tool, neither is it primarily an affective event. Furthermore, it is not and never has been a meal for everyone; it is the meal for those who are already bound to one another in a very specific covenant.

b) We have to be honest in understanding the Eucharist as both a sign of unity and a builder of unity. It is not either/or. Those who see it as a builder of unity are quite right. And if it were only this, then we ought to share it with each other on the way to a fully-realized and universally recognized unity. But if it is also a *sign* of unity, then we cannot share it before we have reached a union that is recognized through the visible and authoritative mechanisms. If I may be permitted a potentially uncomfortable analogy, sex, likewise, builds unity, but belongs properly among people who are in a life-long covenanted bond with each other.

c) We have to identify the offerer of the Eucharist, which is the same as the identity of the One Who is offered: Jesus Christ. This means that questions of exclusion or inclusion at the table are not decided with a pretense to ownership. It is not the Eucharist of the celebrant, of the parish, or of a denomination. In this sense, the expression "eucharistic hospitality" is a misnomer, firstly because it presumes that you or I can be the "hosts" who may choose to offer our personal openness, and secondly because "eucharistic hospitality" misleadingly portrays some churches as "hospitable" and others as "inhospitable," as if it is a question of graciousness.

d) We also have to identify the church. The Eucharist is not ours. It is Christ's; it is his body given for his body the church. So who is the church? Where is the church? Some may answer that the church is the body of faithful Christians, or of baptized Christians, or a body whose actual boundaries are not known. And there is something compelling about these, perhaps especially this last definition. But even as we can retain an apophatic silence about the boundaries of the church known only to God, we have the responsibility of identifying the church as it is revealed to us within history. In Orthodox teaching, the identity and location of the church rests with specific persons—bishops, who are *ex officio* identified with the apostolic faith. That is the tangible and fixed sign of where the church is, and it has been so since the first-century texts of St. Ignatius of Antioch, and in the canonical structures that developed in the immediately ensuing early centuries.

Knowing the identity of the church, and locating it with the bishops in communion with each other, locates where we may partake of the one cup. It is that simple. Otherwise, apart from official inter-church intercommunion agreements, we are left to our own feelings or convictions as to whether or not we share the faith and are united in it. Personally, I feel united in faith with many persons outside my church. I also feel a strong desire to commune at certain celebrations of the Lord's Supper outside my church. But it isn't about what I think, or even what I might demonstrate as a common faith with others. Unity in faith is ephemeral until it is recognized universally, and that universality is signified by the bishop.

I recall Geoffrey Wainwright giving the commencement address at our seminary a couple of years ago. He closed by saying that he had attended the Divine Liturgy together with us all that very morning and could not understand why he could not commune with us. At one level, of course, it is confusing and painful that Geoffrey could not share in the Eucharist with us; we do well to be unsettled by this. But on the other hand, who is in a position to evaluate these things? Geoffrey Wainwright can commune here, while another Methodist with a lower Christology could not?

No one at the Liturgy is there as an *individual*. They are there with their church, *as* their church, with the bishop as the tangible, visible criterion of the church's faith and order and identity. None of this is at the individual level: it is at the ecclesial level, and the bishop, again, identifies ecclesiality.

We know where the church is. We commonly add the apophatic corrective, that we don't know where the church is not. We could say the same about the Eucharist: we know among whom it may be shared. Outside of that, we do not know.

e) "We know where it is, *but not where it isn't.*" That second clause ought also to indicate that our inability to share the Lord's Supper is not a statement about the reality or the efficacy of the Eucharist performed outside the canonical borders of our church. I cannot imagine that God ignores a Lutheran's prayer over the eucharistic gifts and withholds his Holy Spirit from them. But that leads to the next question and the next portion of my presentation.

2. Conceiving the Eucharist

What do the different churches conceive their celebration of the Lord's Supper to be? Are they asking the Holy Spirit to make these gifts to *be* the body and blood of Christ? Are they celebrating a memorial meal in remembrance of Christ's sacrifice? Or some combination? In either case, it is a very good and holy thing to do, but they are different things. And the idea of "sharing" becomes strained, if not absurd, if the different people present understand themselves to be partaking of quite different events, different realities.

As we repeat tirelessly, issues in the sharing and non-sharing of communion have a great deal to do with unity in faith. Apart from a harmonized faith in and teaching about God, about Jesus Christ, about the Trinity, about the nature of the human person, sin, salvation—and you could say that all of this has primarily to do with the teaching about who Jesus Christ is—eucharistic sharing should probably have something to do with a common understanding of what the *Eucharist* actually is. Even as we retain a sense of mystery about this holy rite, in some of our churches we approach it with some palpably different assumptions. Should we share it if we think such different things about what we are actually sharing?

There have been old and new discussions about this. There has been Calvin versus Zwingli. We have seen the *realiter non mystice,* and the *mystice non realiter.* Churches and theologians have discussed "real presence," "transubstantiation," "sign," "symbol," "memorial," "sacrifice," or "anamnesis." Each church, and to a certain extent different theologians within the churches, configure these terms and ideas variously. It would be possible to identify important areas of agreement, as well as significant points of real division, and the 1982 BEM document[2] has been enormously helpful in indicating some of each.

The Orthodox, for their part, have invoked virtually all of the terms that have been put into play in Christian thinking on the Eucharist. Looking at Fr. Alexander Schmemann's final work, *The Eucharist*,[3] we will see many familiar ideas configured in a particular way and sometimes leading to new and fresh places. We see the Eucharist understood as anamnesis, we see the importance of the preached word. We also see the centrality of the gathering itself. In fact, one of the main points of the book is to show that the presence of Christ cannot be pinpointed to one place, one moment, one exclamation—it is the entire Liturgy and even that which precedes and follows it.[4] The epiclesis is central, of course, but we take note that the we call on God to send his Holy Spirit "upon *us* and upon these gifts set forth."

Several Christian traditions (sometimes following Schmemann and sometimes preceding and influencing him) have adopted this same kind of holistic understanding, one that does not undermine the particularity of the eucharistic gifts. Schmemann uses the word "symbol" as well, to describe the relationship between the gifts and Christ. But as ever, one has to define "symbol." And he comes up with a robust definition, where (with the help of etymology) he speaks of "symbol" as the "throwing together" of two realities, the one not merely indicating the other but participating in it.[5] So none of the terms or ideas themselves (memorial, symbol, preached word) are taboo for Orthodox. It is a matter of configuration.

Orthodox in history have even used the scholasticized language of "transubstantiation" and "substance/accidents," in settings as significant as the Synod of Jerusalem in 1672. But this usage is reluctant, the terminology is invoked grudgingly: the very same synod states explicitly that these words cannot be understood definitively or technically. Schmemann, again, speaks for many in the Orthodox Church when he says that "any attempt

---

2. *Baptism, Eucharist, and Ministry* (Faith and Order Paper No. 111), 1982. Online: http://www.oikoumene.org/en/resources/documents/wcc-commissions/faith-and-order-commission/i-unity-the-church-and-its-mission/baptism-eucharist-and-ministry-faith-and-order-paper-no-111-the-lima-text.html.

3. *The Eucharist: Sacrament of the Kingdom* (Crestwood, NY: St. Vladimir's Seminary Press, 1988).

4. Ibid. Cf. especially 162–64.

5. Ibid., 38.

to *explain* the conversion, to locate it in formulas and clauses, is not only unnecessary but truly harmful."[6]

I would agree, as I imagine that many of us would, about the potential harmfulness of excessive prying into these mysteries to discern their precise ontological status. As C. S. Lewis memorably said about the Last Supper, "The command, after all, was Take, eat: not Take, understand."[7] Yet the debates do leave us with an unanswered question about the nature of the *stuff* that we partake of at our celebrations of the Lord's Supper: is it sacred? Or is it the whole event that is sacred? Or are *both* sacred, though perhaps in a different way?

Here too we could go around in circles about what we mean by "sacred," and some of that debate has certainly been had about "sacrament," a word that is used in some churches (with a degree of variation in meaning) and avoided in others.[8] But it seems that apart from asking what people think happens to the bread and the wine, or other elements that might be used, we might learn a lot more and learn it more quickly if we ask what people *do* with these elements—before, during, and after the celebration of the Eucharist. As they say, deeds prove dispositions. Or if I may adapt an old adage, "sacred is as sacred does."

3. Handling the Eucharist

In describing some of the different practices as I am about to do, I have no intention to evaluate them as good or as bad, as wise or unwise. *They are what they are meant to be, without apology or compromise, within each tradition.* But as such, they serve as faithful barometers of people's corporate or ecclesial sense about what Holy Communion is. And to the extent there is agreement or disagreement on these things, we might learn something about the sharing and non-sharing of the Supper.

My observations of the various practices come from conversations with friends across the ecumenical spectrum, rather than from academic or ecclesiastical texts. My hope is that this will not weaken but in fact enhance the goals of this inquiry, which are phenomenological in nature,

---

6. Ibid., 222.

7. *Letters to Malcolm, Chiefly on Prayer* (New York: Mariner, 2002) 104.

8. See Peter Bouteneff, "The Mystery of Union: Elements in an Orthodox Sacramental Theology," in *Gestures of God: Explorations in Sacramental Theology*, ed. Geoffrey Rowell and Christine Hall (New York: Continuum, 2004) 91–107.

being about on-the-ground praxis rather than theory. I will summarize approaches from four churches that might represent a helpful though far from a complete spectrum: Disciples of Christ, Lutheran, Orthodox, and Roman Catholic. In each case we will look at the handling of the elements with a few words about eucharistic piety and a short and basic explanation of rationale.

Christian Church (Disciples of Christ)

Disciples are of considerable interest to this inquiry because although they are a "low church" denomination emerging from the Restoration movement, and although they are congregational by nature, they are one of the Reformed traditions that "do this" (i.e., celebrate the Lord's Supper) with frequency and regularity: as often as they interpret scripture. Michael Kinnamon, drawing on an interesting personal anecdote, famously called his church "A People Obsessed with Bread."[9]

So Disciples take communion seriously and often. As to the elements of communion and their handling, there is a broad diversity of practices and no single prescribed liturgical book. There is no hard and fast rule that the elements should be bread and wine. A majority of congregations would use juice, others would use wine. For the bread, some use communion wafers, others yeasted bread. In some cases, such as at youth groups and camps, goldfish crackers and grape Kool-Aid have been used as a sign of the contextual nature of faith and liturgy.

At no point in the table prayers—or before or after—is a substantive reverence shown to the elements themselves. This is because what is being consecrated is the gathering. The Eucharist is not in the elements but in the gathering and in the action. Afterwards, the elements are treated in no special way. They may be served at a fellowship hour, or sent home with parishioners; it would not be unheard of to dispose of them. The point, again, is to focus on the act rather than on the elements.

9. "A People Obsessed with Bread: Images of Disciples' Identity and Mission," *Lexington Theological Quarterly* 28 (1993) 85–95.

Evangelical Lutheran Church

Most Lutheran churches use ordinary yeasted bread, some use communion wafers. In any case neither the bread nor the wine (or grape juice) is specifically blessed or treated in some special way beforehand.

During the service, the bread and wine are from the beginning on the altar table, covered. The bread is prepared before the service begins, roughly in accordance with the number of people present. The practice of what to do with any leftovers varies considerably from place to place, and in many (though not all) churches there is an attempt to handle them with reverence and care; some texts will even specify this. Traditionally the idea was to use the leftovers for the communion of the sick, but this practice has become very rare. Some pastors will consume the leftovers after the service, sharing them with the people who had a function in the service. It is sometimes advised to "give the elements back to the earth which gave them to us," in other words, the rest of the wine would be poured into the earth (especially if it is too much to be consumed after the service), and the bread taken home and eaten with the family.

The tradition of confession of sins before partaking of Holy Communion has largely fallen away, having been seen as casting to negative an atmosphere on the event. Yet a spirit of reverence, for the event and for the things partaken of, remains.

Orthodox Church (Chalcedonian)

In the Orthodox Church, exclusively yeasted bread is used. It is usually fresh baked: there are websites about the preparation of "prosphora" bread and its history, taking note also of saints who are associated with the baking of this bread.[10]

The celebration of the Eucharist is preceded by a set service of preparation in which the carving of the bread and the prayers said at every stage are meticulously scripted. The bread is apportioned in memory of different persons and events; the preparation service is one of "gathering" of people living or departed, which parallels the gathering of people coming to church.

The elements are from this point onward treated with great reverence and care. After the Liturgy of the Word they are processed solemnly from

10. See, for example, www.prosphora.org.

the table of preparation to the altar table—a procession so elaborate and storied as to have merited a five-hundred-page study by Robert Taft.[11]

There is always an epiclesis, calling down the Holy Spirit "upon us, and upon these gifts here set forth." At the same time, especially through the liturgical renewal of the late twentieth century, a more holistic understanding of Christ's presence at/in the Eucharist has taken precedence over the idea of a single moment of transformation.

The elements are all consumed. Anything left over following the communion of the faithful is consumed by the clergy, down to the very last crumb or particle, or taken to the sick. The consecrated gifts exist only to be eaten.

Communion is always preceded by a complete fast from food and from sexual activity. Communicants are required to be involved in a regular discipline of confession.

Roman Catholic Church

In the Roman Catholic Church, unyeasted bread—communion wafers—are used. These and the wine do not receive particularly elaborate reverence or ceremony before their consecration. After the Liturgy of the Word, the bread and wine are processed, often by members of the congregation, sometimes together with the financial offering, and the gifts are placed upon the altar. A brief prayer is said over them.

There is a clear point of demarcation at the words of institution, which is the moment when the elements become the body and blood of Christ. In some celebrations of the Mass there will also be an epiclesis.

Clergy (or at least the presider) partake of both bread and wine; the congregation usually only partakes of the bread. Leftover elements are all consumed with care or reserved for the sick, never disposed of.

Confession before communion is common, and it is required in the case of mortal sins. A sexual fast is traditional, while fasting from food has been reduced to one hour before partaking.

In speaking about the treatment of the eucharistic elements, I would take note of one further rite often celebrated in the Roman Catholic Church, as well as in some Anglican and Lutheran churches, but not in the Orthodox

11. *The Great Entrance: A History of the Transfer of Gifts and Other Pre-anaphoral Rites of the Liturgy of St. John Chrysostom* (Rome: Pontificium Institutum Studiorum Orientalium, 1975).

Church: the adoration of the blessed host, where the people show reverence for the consecrated host, and are blessed by it, without eating it.[12]

Implications

We are getting a sense of some common points as well as differences. The differences of how we handle the elements are important, and have been for at least a millennium and a half. The fifth-century christological controversy between Cyril and Nestorius had profound implications for the Eucharist.[13] Later on, in the eleventh century, it may seem strange to us today that the greatest controversy that rocked Christendom, the dispute at the heart of what prompted the papal bull of excommunication in 1054, was the disagreement as to whether to use yeasted or unyeasted (azyme) bread in the Eucharist.[14] One patriarch of Antioch wrote, "The matter of azymes involves in summary form the whole question of true piety."[15] The azyme controversy cut to Christology as well as anthropology. That is how important "what we do *with* this" has been in church history.

I would contest that it is still extremely important today, and that is because what we do stems from what we believe: *Lex panis lex est credendi*! A division in eucharistic practice and piety likely points to a different understanding of the Eucharist. Some of these differences are incremental, some of them are major.

In some cases we are talking about quite different events, about meals of a very different nature. It is difficult or impossible to conceive of "eucharistic sharing" in cases where one church consumes the gifts with utmost reverence and care and the other, owing to their understanding, sees no problem with throwing the unused elements away. These are two very different "things" being consumed, at celebrations that have a radically different meaning to the people present. Non-sharing in such cases isn't

12. On the rationale behind the Orthodox rejection of this practice, see Alexander Schmemann, *Great Lent* (Crestwood, NY: St. Vladimir's Seminary Press, 1969) 59.

13. Henry Chadwick, "Eucharist and Christology in the Nestorian Controversy," *Journal of Theological Studies*, n.s. 2 (1951) 145–64.

14. John H. Erickson, "Leavened and Unleavened: Some Theological Implications of the Schism of 1054," *St. Vladimir's Theological Quarterly* 14 (1970) 3–24; reprinted in *The Challenge of Our Past: Studies in Orthodox Canon Law and Church History* (Crestwood, NY: St. Vladimir's Seminary Press, 1991) 133–55. (Page references in the present essay are taken from the latter.)

15. See ibid., 134.

exclusion, it is merely respecting reality. In such cases it seems to me that *sharing* would be scandalous, for all who are present. Not because of what some might consider to be inscrutable differences in doctrine, but because of the basic fact of conceiving the meal so differently.

It may be asked: why would an Orthodox Christian find it impossible to eat at the Lord's Supper in a setting where the bread and wine are understood explicitly as tokens, to which no change happens? If everyone agrees that this is just bread, without the pretense of being anything else, what's the problem in sharing it? The problem is that we are still talking about "doing this," probably invoking words of institution, words that have a very different valence for those present. With any event of this kind, you are entering what we see as sacramental territory, whether or not you conceive it so. Furthermore, our sharing would convey a misleading sign of unity in faith among our churches. Recall that we are there not as individuals, but as our churches.

Conclusions and Suggestions

It is commonly noted that the divergences within some of the churches are greater than the divergences between them. I would further say that the diversity of positions within many of the churches is a factor that divides them from each other, and certainly from the Orthodox Church. This applies also to what we believe about the Lord's Supper, and what happens at our celebrations of it. The Orthodox Church is not a monolith of faith positions and of practices but its diversity is of an entirely different scale from that in many if not most other churches. The wide scope of faith positions and liturgical and eucharistic pieties *within* some of the denominations is testimony to an ecclesiology and eucharistic understanding very different from that of the Orthodox Church. It is the same with some of the unity agreements that have been reached, for example between churches with an episcopate in the apostolic succession, and those without one. Their very unity, in the face of that difference, testifies to an ecclesiology that differs significantly from ours.[16]

In the face of all that unites the great Christian traditions, the evident fact remains that we are not unified in faith. This means we must reconsider

16. See Peter Bouteneff, "The Porvoo Common Statement: An Orthodox Response," in *Apostolicity and Unity: Essays on the Porvoo Common Statement*, ed. Ola Tjørhom (Grand Rapids: Eerdmans, 2002) 231–44.

where we locate the scandal of an unshared Eucharist: the scandal actually lies in the disunity that *precedes* and often rightly leads to the unshared Eucharist. Not sharing the Eucharist might, for many reasons, be appropriate and I dare say even salutary. It is a sharp reminder that all is not well with us, that we have work to do before we are united to one another.

Some of the divided churches are considerably closer to each other in faith and in their understanding of the Lord's Supper, and the idea of their sharing it is less difficult to swallow, as it were. But even here, I might make the deeply unpopular suggestion . . .of not sharing until there is a fully-realized and recognized unity in faith and ministry. Consider it not an exclusion, or a rejection, but as a *fast*. Until we can do this right, and permanently, let's humbly abstain, in mutual respect. A fast from intercommunion would be very difficult to implement and to explain to each other. But it may be that a lovingly-conceived abstention would goad us to work for genuine unity in faith and in order. Otherwise we will be tempted to say "It is enough that we commune with each other. We needn't to go the full mile of reconciliation."

Take or leave this suggestion of the intercommunion fast. But I do hope I have managed to convey a sense of the Orthodox logic of communion and intercommunion and that I have been true to it. The intention here has been to take us beyond the idea that sharing the Eucharist is a sign of openness and graciousness, while not sharing it comes from obstinacy and theological obsession. This may be hard to believe, especially when we are ungracious in our behavior. But the actual rationale needs to be explained.

I would like to close by offering what might be a more palatable suggestion: a recommendation with an ecumenical pedigree. The BEM document liked to confront differences by naming them, describing them, and then by assigning each side of the difference to consider something about the other side. The Eucharist section of BEM is helpful in summarizing and moving forward on convergences and divergences in eucharistic concept and piety. When it comes to the issue discussed in the present essay, here is what it says:

> 32. Some churches stress that Christ's presence in the consecrated elements continues after the celebration. Others place the main emphasis on the act of celebration itself and on the consumption of the elements in the act of communion. The way in which the elements are treated requires special attention. Regarding the

practice of reserving the elements, each church should respect the practices and piety of the others. Given the diversity in practice among the churches and at the same time taking note of the present situation in the convergence process, it is worthwhile to suggest:

- that, on the one hand, it be remembered, especially in sermons and instruction, that the primary intention of reserving the elements is their distribution among the sick and those who are absent, and

- on the other hand, it be recognized that the best way of showing respect for the elements served in the eucharistic celebration is by their consumption, without excluding their use for communion of the sick.

Might we extend these recommendations along the following lines?

Those with a sacramental understanding of the Eucharist are encouraged to consider the reverent beauty and uncluttered faithfulness of the memorial meal celebrated in churches without a sacramental theology. Those without a theology of sacrament are encouraged to consider the implications of a more "transformative" understanding of the elements, beginning perhaps with a reflection on how the word "symbol" is being understood. And all are encouraged to revere and love the things of the Lord's table. Not fetishizing them. But not disposing of them. Eating them, as the Lord commanded, "Take, eat."

Practices and attitudes evolve. Confession, fasting, and other dimensions of eucharistic piety and practice have declined in many places, and they are capable of coming back: might contemporary Methodists seek to retrieve Charles Wesley's hymns on the Lord's Supper? In some churches communion pieties were abandoned deliberately in reaction to excesses, and may now be ripe for reconsideration: might the Restoration churches explore other ways of understanding "This is my body" and what it may imply for "this" bread today? The point is, what we believe influences what we do, but it works the other way around as well. If everyone treats these things with a converging reverence, we may be directing ourselves towards greater unity in faith about what they are, and thus moving towards being able to partake of them together in unity.

5

Eucharist: The Table That Unites and Divides the Church

Martha Moore-Keish

Introduction

When I received the invitation to speak at this gathering, the organizers offered a couple of guiding questions: how does the Eucharist reflect, express,
or realize what it means to be church? And how could our celebrations of
the Supper better relate to our being as church? In other words, what is the
relationship between the table and the church, and how can we be better at
both? I will reflect on this question in three parts:

- What does it mean to be church? As a part of this, what do the "creedal
  marks" suggest about the nature of the church?

- Focus on the mark of the church as "one"—and how has the Eucharist
  expressed and obscured this? In other words, how has the table both
  united and divided the church?

- Finally, how might our celebrations of the Lord's Supper better express
  the unity (rather the disunity) of the church?

1. What Does It Mean to Be "Church"?

The church is an eccentric people. Now, this is probably not news to any of you who are here, whether you are long time church members or some kind of professional leaders of churches. The church is eccentric. Let me tell you what I mean.

David Kelsey, longtime professor of theology at Yale Divinity School (now retired), published in 2009 his magnum opus on theological anthropology, a two-volume work titled *Eccentric Existence*. If you have read it, or read a review of it, you know that Kelsey argues in that work that human beings are fundamentally ec-centric beings—that is, our centers are not in ourselves, but outside of ourselves. We do not find our core identities in ourselves; we find them in another—namely, in the triune God. Our very existence in every dimension can only be understood by looking to the One whose breath, time, and life define our own.

Kelsey's book is a remarkable achievement, and I commend it to you. For the purposes of our discussion today, however, I am simply borrowing his fundamental insight about human beings and applying it to the church: we are eccentric, centered not in ourselves, but in God. Or, as Calvin put it in talking about the Christian life, "we are not our own; we belong to God."

If we investigate the meaning of the word "church" itself, we get a glimpse of this eccentric identity. The Greek term *ekklesia* (which we translate "church") means those who are "called out." That is, the very term used to name the Christian community implies that the church is dependent for its very existence on the call, the summons, of another. According to Hans Küng in his classic book *The Church*, *ekklesia* in the New Testament refers to the eschatological people of God, who have heard and responded to Jesus' proclamation of God's coming reign of righteousness and peace.[1] We, heirs of that people, are likewise called out to live in light of that coming reign, in time borrowed from the future, embodied here and now.

So too the word "church" shows our eccentric existence. The English word "church" comes from the German *kirche*, which itself goes back to another Greek term, *kyriakon*: "that which belongs to the Lord." Both of these terms, *ekklesia* and *kyriakon*, suggest that we are a peculiar kind of people, who do not gather ourselves but are called by another. (Incidentally, this is why when we begin our worship services with a "call to worship," it is vital to recall that it is God who calls us to worship, not we ourselves.) We are a

---

1. Hans Küng, *The Church* (London: Burns & Oates, 1968) 83.

community that belongs not to itself but to God. And the church's identity is therefore "ec-centric," founded not in itself and its own call, but in the call of and communion with the triune God.

All of that might sound terribly abstract. What does it look like to find our identity not in ourselves but in the call of and communion with the triune God? Since its earliest days, the church has embodied its ec-centric faith in certain core practices: proclaiming and hearing together the word of God through the writings of Hebrew scripture and the apostolic teaching (which together we commonly call "the Bible"); baptizing people as a sign of entrance into the community of Christ; praying together through Jesus to the one whom he called "Father"; sharing in fellowship and ministering to those in need; and, most importantly for our purposes today, breaking bread and sharing the cup in a meal variously called the Lord's Supper, Eucharist, communion.

Why has this particular practice been so important to the church's life? First, because meals were central to Jesus' ministry. You cannot miss this when you read through the gospels. He eats with Pharisees, with "tax collectors and sinners," as well as with his own disciples; he feeds the four thousand and the five thousand; he tells parables about the kingdom of heaven as a great dinner or a wedding banquet; he describes himself as "the bread of life"; he shares a meal with his disciples on the night before he is betrayed. And, according to Luke and John, after his resurrection, he shared meals again with his disciples (so that the so-called last supper really isn't). Jesus broke bread with Cleopas and his companion in the town of Emmaus, and shared a breakfast of bread and fish with Peter and six others on the shore of the sea of Tiberias. Apparently, Jesus' followers so identified him with the practice of breaking bread together that this act caused their "eyes to be opened" so that they could recognize him when they met him again in his risen form.

It is no surprise, then, that breaking and sharing bread and cup became a central part of Christian worship from the beginning. In the book of Acts, right after Pentecost, Luke describes the life of the earliest converts: "They devoted themselves to the apostles' teaching and fellowship, to the breaking of bread and the prayers" (Acts 2:42). This gave a thumbnail sketch of the basic features of earliest Christian worship: hearing the teaching of the apostles (first orally, and later in written form), being together in fellowship, sharing a meal, and offering prayers. The meal was a core practice, after the practice that was at the core of Jesus' own ministry.

Notice this: sharing the Lord's Supper was central to church practice not just because people liked to eat together, but because in that breaking of bread and sharing of the cup, they met and pledged their loyalty to someone beyond themselves: their risen Lord. By calling it "the Lord's Supper" from the beginning, they announced that they, and their meal, were not their own. The Supper (at its best) embodies in practice the church's eccentric identity.

As early Christians continued to break bread together, they also began to reflect on who they were as the gathered followers of Jesus. What was this movement that they began to call "church"? From early on, Christians began to describe the church's identity using four terms. As the Nicene Creed puts it, the church is "one, holy, catholic, and apostolic." These are not sociological descriptions, but theological claims about the church's "eccentric" identity which is beyond itself, in God. Briefly: our holiness is derivative—dependent on God, who alone is truly holy. The church is holy only insofar as the Holy Spirit moves within it. Our catholicity, the wholeness of the church into which we are incorporated, is never fully realized in our own life together, but is found only in Christ. And the apostolicity of the church defines the church as those who are sent out—αποστελλο. The church is apostolic because it is sent by God, who set the church in motion and continues to power the church's life today. Each mark of the church directs (or should direct) our gaze beyond ourselves, to the triune one who alone is holy, whole, and sending.

But today we focus on the first mark: the unity of the church. What does it mean to call the church "one," and how has the Lord's Supper, the Eucharist, expressed and obscured this mark of the church?

2. How Has the Eucharist Expressed and Obscured the Unity of the Church?

Let's back up for a moment. Why did "the breaking of the bread" have such basic significance to those early Christians? Because it connected them with Jesus, of course, with his own meals during his life, at his death, and after his resurrection. That much we have said already. But what is it about eating and drinking together that carries such power, so that meals became so central to Jesus' own identity? To begin with, there is the obvious fact that we require food to live. We need nourishment, sustenance, simply to continue breathing and walking on this earth. This may be obvious, but we should not skip over it too quickly. The table is about feeding us, and thus it discloses us as vulnerable, needy creatures. Food signals that we are dependent on something outside of ourselves for life itself. So when Jesus says "I am the bread of life," it connects deeply with this most primal need.

But there is more. Sharing meals, after all, is not just about satisfying our own hunger and thirst. "Breaking bread" was and is about gathering together around a common table, acknowledging the humanity of the others who are there, and acknowledging our common vulnerability. If we eat together, we proclaim that we are all equally dependent on something outside ourselves for life. If we pass the bread basket to the person next to us, we are in effect saying, "I see you, and I know that you too are hungry. Rather than eating all of these biscuits myself, I am going to share some with you." Unless we are just sitting side by side at a table, eating our own separate meals and connected to our separate iPods, gathering around food and drink declares that we have a relationship, that we have mutual regard for one another.

This means that when we come to the Eucharist, we proclaim our unity in the very fact of eating and drinking together. Our table practices can contribute to the unity of the church when we more fully embody this celebration as an actual meal, because in this way, we proclaim our common hunger, and our common humanity.

In Jesus' day, sharing meals was a significant way of acknowledging the common humanity of others. As we know, social rules around meal sharing were more stringent then than they are for most of us today. People did not sit at table with others of a different social class, or with any they regarded as "unclean." This is why it was so shocking for Jesus to eat with "tax collectors," who were regarded by observant Jews of the time as traitors, accomplices of the Roman government, who took money from their own people to support the foreign empire. Some think that it was his "open table" practices, above all, that got him into trouble with the authorities, ultimately leading to his trial and execution. He sat at table with anybody, apparently, willing to break bread and pass the cup even with "sinners," with those who had not kept the law, with betrayers like Zacchaeus. And Judas. And Peter.

The table of the Lord, from the beginning, has carried with it this additional, disconcerting aspect of our unity: not only are we all equally in need of nourishment, but we are all equally in need of mercy. Jesus sits at table not with the righteous, but with sinners—that is, us. So meal sharing was a powerful demonstration of Jesus' message: about our common hunger, our common humanity, *and our common need for forgiveness.* This is worth pondering as we come to the table today; do we celebrate the Eucharist in a way that evades our need of forgiveness, or that implies that some are more sinful than others? How might we proclaim more clearly at table our unity *as sinners* dependent on the Lord's grace?

Though Christians from the beginning regarded the meal as central to their gatherings, we know that it did not take any time at all for divisions to arise. Paul's first letter to the church in Corinth, which gives such a clarion call to unity at the table, also gives us a clear glimpse of division: "When you come together, it is not really to eat the Lord's Supper," he says. "For when the time comes to eat, each of you goes ahead with your own supper, and one goes hungry and another becomes drunk. What? Do you not have homes to eat and drink in? Or do you show contempt for the church of God and humiliate those who have nothing?" In Corinth, the problem seems to be class division: some have more, others have less, and they have overlooked what Paul regards as central to Jesus' teaching: that this meal is about sharing in common. All have need. All are hungry. To allow some to go without food is to deny Jesus yet again.

Ever since Corinth, Christians have continued to have divisions at the table, even as we continue to proclaim and long for unity. One issue that has sparked heated debate since at least the ninth century is this: what does it mean when Jesus said "this is my body . . . this is my blood"? Some Christians have emphasized the direct, even literal identification of the bread and wine with the body and blood of Christ. Cyril of Jerusalem in the fourth century explained this to some newly baptized Christians, saying, "Let us partake with the fullest confidence that it is the body and blood of Christ. For his body has been bestowed on you in the form of bread, and his blood in the form of wine, so that by partaking of Christ's body and blood you may share with him the same body and blood." Cyril continues, "This is how we become bearers of Christ, since his body and blood spreads throughout our limbs; this is how, in the blessed Peter's words, 'we become partakers of the divine nature.'"[2] For Cyril, the bread and wine must be literally the body and blood of Christ, because this is the way we are directly united with his life. We take his body into ours, and we are thus changed.

2. Cyril of Jerusalem, "Sermon 4: The Eucharist," in *The Awe-Inspiring Rites of Initiation: The Origins of the R.C.I.A.*, ed. Edward Yarnold, 2nd ed. (Collegeville, MN: Liturgical, 1994) 86–87.

When Cyril taught this in the fourth century, it was not particularly controversial. However, in the ninth century, a Frankish monk named Paschasius Radbertus taught something very similar, and it did start an argument. Radbertus wrote that the literal, historical body of Christ was present in the bread of the Eucharist—the same body that was "born of Mary, suffered on the cross, and was raised from the dead," as he put it. Like Cyril, Radbertus argued this point because he saw it as essential to understanding our salvation. By taking the body of Christ into ourselves, we are truly united with him and his life.

Another monk at the same monastery was infuriated by Radbertus's explanation. Ratramnus of Corbie wrote a treatise with the same name as Radbertus's: *De corpore et sanguine Domini* (*On the Body and Blood of the Lord*). In it, Ratramnus maintained that the bread and wine are not the actual body and blood of the Christ of history, but are "symbols of remembrance." Through them, the Holy Spirit joins a person to Christ in a real but invisible way.[3] The two brother monks agreed on a lot: at the Eucharist, the real presence of Christ was received by the faithful through the power of the Spirit. But Ratramnus denied that what the faithful received was the historical, literal body of Christ. So, eventually, his essay was condemned and burned by a church council in 1050 and nearly forgotten until the sixteenth century, at which point some Protestants became very interested in its argument, so close to some of their own.

So the argument has gone. Roman Catholic theologians, and Luther in his own way, argue that Christ is really present in the bread and wine. From the thirteenth century forward, this affirmation has been linked to the concept of transubstantiation, the philosophical account of the conversion of the substance of the bread and wine into the substance of Christ's body and blood. Meanwhile Zwingli and many other Reformed theologians insist on a strong distinction between the bread and the body. If Christ is present, it is through our remembrance of him as we gather at table. Still others, like Calvin, have tried to seek a middle way in the debate, and have been misunderstood and maligned by both sides in the process. Calvin described Christ as being "truly present" by the power of the Spirit, but not in a local or substantial way. The contentious debate over how to interpret the simple word "is" in the statement "this IS my body" continues to be one of

3. *The New Schaff-Herzog Encyclopedia of Religious Knowledge*, ed. Samuel Macauley Jackson (Grand Rapids: Baker, 1953) 9:403.

the deepest divides in eucharistic theology today (though, as I will suggest later, there has been some recent progress).

What does this debate reveal about the unity of the church? Not much. Except this: the oneness of the church does not reside, and will never reside, in our theological agreement. If we try to make our efforts at understanding the basis of our unity, we will forever be disappointed. This is not an argument against ecumenical dialogue, which is after all one of our purposes in gathering here. But it is an argument for humility—and eccentric faith. Better to think of the church, as Kathryn Tanner and others have suggested, as a community of argument. This means that our unity can be glimpsed not in absolute agreement, but in a common focus on that which is outside of ourselves, which we see only in part. We argue about important things— where is Christ when we come to the table? How is the Spirit at work here? But it is those things that unite us, not our answers, not our common understanding of what they mean.

Here is another issue that has divided Christians at the table: what does it mean to eat and drink the Lord's Supper "in an unworthy manner"? This line from 1 Corinthians 11 has haunted Christian communities for centuries. Does it mean that we need to confess our sins and receive forgiveness before coming to the table? Does it mean that we need to fast and pray in preparation? Does it mean that we need to have a clear understanding of who Christ is in order to receive the elements faithfully? Who is worthy to eat and drink at the Lord's Supper—and who decides?

This has been a particular concern in my own tradition of Reformed Protestantism. At their best, efforts to encourage "worthy participation" were intended to maintain Christian accountability to one another. This is what the church leaders in Geneva were trying to do when they set up the consistory under John Calvin in the sixteenth century. It is difficult for us independent-minded Americans to imagine living with the constant oversight of a body charged with the ordering of community life, with the power to call people to account for marital disputes, quarreling, doctrinal error, or failure to attend public worship. Yet the primary work of the consistory was to ensure that the citizens of Geneva showed some consistency between their worship and the rest of their lives; or, to put it another way, they wanted the Genevans to live so that they could worthily participate in the Lord's Supper.

The consistory focused on a variety of cases, and their work changed somewhat over the years. In the beginning they spent much of their time trying to ensure that everyone in Geneva could recite the Lord's Prayer and Apostles' Creed in French, rather than Latin. Later, the consistory spent more time trying to resolve interpersonal and communal problems among Genevan citizens. This is particularly worth noting: people were expected to be reconciled to one another in order to participate in the Lord's Supper. The emphasis on "worthy participation in the Supper" had primarily to do with forgiving and being reconciled. To be sure, the consistory did exercise excommunication as the ultimate penalty for unfaithful behavior, but this was usually a temporary condition, meant to prompt repentance and restoration to the community. As historian Elsie Anne McKee notes, "In the week before the celebration of the Lord's Supper there were always extra Consistory meetings with the specific purpose of giving those who were suspended an opportunity to express their repentance and be reconciled, and so to demonstrate their worthiness for admission to the Lord's Supper."[4] Nevertheless, we can be sure that some Genevan citizens did not see it this way, but instead received the rebuke of the consistory as a denial of Christ's welcome to sinners to break bread with him.

What might we learn about the unity of the church from the Genevan consistory and its focus on worthy participation? Many things could be said here, but I will focus on just one: this attention to real reconciliation prior to participation in the Supper underscored the significance of the Eucharist as a meal of genuine unity. The meal was not simply the appearance of unity; it was to be a meal of those who had truly been reconciled. Now, I do not want to minimize the difficulty of living this out in practice, and the way in which it can and has led to abuse of power. But just imagine what it would be like in your congregation if sisters and brothers who were quarreling had to admit the ways they had hurt each other, and seek forgiveness, before sharing the bread and the cup. Just imagine the way the meal could be a celebration of broken relationships now healed. Paul wrote, "all who eat and drink without discerning the body, eat and drink judgment against themselves." (1 Cor 11:29) Our unity lies in Christ, but we are called to reflect that unity, even in a dim, fragmentary way, in our own relations to one another.

The struggle over how to hold together "worthy participation" in the Supper with hunger for the grace of Jesus Christ who ate with sinners can

---

4. Elsie Anne McKee, "General Introduction," in *John Calvin: Writings on Pastoral Piety*, ed. and trans. Elsie Anne McKee, Classics of Western Spirituality (New York: Paulist, 2001) 17.

also be seen in the early history of Reformed Protestants in this country. Over the course of the seventeenth century, Puritans in New England came to emphasize holiness of life as a prerequisite to participation in the sacraments. That is, only people who were obviously "regenerate" (made new through God's grace) were true members of the covenant, and could therefore be admitted to baptism and the Lord's Supper. Many church leaders required an account of personal experience of saving grace in order to be considered "regenerate."

The so-called halfway covenant of 1662 relaxed these expectations a bit, requiring an account of an experience of grace in order to join a church and receive communion, but allowing children and grandchildren of members to be baptized even if they had not made such profession. So while only full members could come to the table, access to baptism was much more open. The effect of this was to make baptism into a sacrament of grace and the Lord's Supper into a sacrament of holiness. Anyone up to the third generation could be admitted to baptism, but only those who examined themselves and were godly persons could come to the table. Solomon Stoddard, pastor at the church in Northampton, Massachusetts, saw this as a problem and tried to ease the restrictions around the table. In the late seventeenth and early eighteenth centuries, Stoddard argued that those who were admitted to baptism also ought to be admitted to the Lord's Supper. Only moral sincerity was necessary; the sacrament of communion itself was a means of grace that could bring those of sincere heart to full conversion. In this way, he hoped to encourage those who were refraining from the Lord's Supper to come back to this "converting ordinance."[5]

Solomon Stoddard's grandson, Jonathan Edwards, initially agreed with his grandfather's approach to the sacraments. Sometime before 1749, however, he changed his mind. Frustrated with the congregation in Northampton, where he had succeeded his grandfather as pastor, he became convinced that allowing those who simply had "moral sincerity" to participate in communion and have their children baptized was contributing to spiritual complacency and even moral hypocrisy in the church. He therefore declared, in February 1749, that he would admit to full communion only those who are "in profession, and in the eye of the church's

---

5. The foregoing paragraph is adapted from David D. Hall's introduction to Jonathan Edwards, *Ecclesiastical Writings*, ed. David D. Hall, Works of Jonathan Edwards 12 (New Haven: Yale University Press, 1994) esp. 19–43.

Christian judgment, godly or gracious persons."[6] This meant that in order to come to the table, receive adult baptism, or have one's children baptized, it was necessary to make a credible public profession of saving faith. The church rebelled, and in the fall of 1750, Edwards was relieved of his pastoral duties at Northampton.

Now, you may not find that little scrap of history as fascinating as I do, but I hope you see at least this much: Christians have been concerned for a long time about what it takes to participate worthily in the sacrament. In the seventeenth and eighteenth centuries, the debate was about whether regeneration should precede participation in the Lord's Supper, or whether the Supper itself might contribute to such conversion to new life. Edwards was trying to embody the conviction that the church is *ekklesia, kyriakon*, those called out, who belong to the Lord. He believed wholeheartedly that the church does not belong to itself, but belongs to God. But unfortunately, his attempt to secure the holiness of the church had the effect of jeopardizing its visible unity.

This historical development reveals a problem about the Eucharist and the unity of the church. I have argued that the church is ec-centric, that our oneness is not to be found in ourselves, but in God. Yet how do we develop practices that can form people in such ec-centric faith? How do we attend carefully to symbolic practices in a way that leads beyond the practices themselves, to the triune Holy One? Edwards is an example of this problem: he enforced public profession of faith as a prerequisite to the table, and in so doing he intended to point to faith in God. But in the process, he managed instead to focus attention on the boundary rather than the center.

How might our own eucharistic practices point to the unity of the church? If Edwards at this point is a cautionary example, then we do better to focus our attention on the strong central symbols and keep our attention there, rather than on patrolling the borders. The unity of the church cannot be enforced by strategies of limit and control. So proclaim the good news with vivid clarity. Invite the congregation to proclaim together the faith we share in the triune God. Celebrate the meal with symbols and gestures that speak clearly of the astonishing mercy of God. And let the people come. Our unity will emerge as we are drawn outside of ourselves by such compelling witness to Christ's work in the world.

6. Ibid., 17; cf. Edwards, "Inquiry Concerning Qualifications for Communion," in ibid., 174.

We have been exploring some major eucharistic questions that have divided the church over the centuries: what does it mean to say that Christ is present when we celebrate the Lord's Supper? and what does it mean to celebrate the Supper worthily? In both cases, though the debates themselves have divided Christians from one another, I have suggested that they provide important insights about the ec-centric unity of the church. Before concluding, I would like to shift attention to some recent ecumenical developments that actually seek the visible unity of the church, and ask again what we might learn there about the Eucharist and the oneness of the church.

For six years, from 2003 to 2010, I served on the national ecumenical dialogue between four Reformed churches in this country and the U.S. Conference of Catholic Bishops. We were charged to explore issues of both baptism and eucharist, and we produced two documents: "These Living Waters" and "This Bread of Life." The second of these focused on the Lord's Supper and includes significant insights on points of convergence, as well as clarifying points of continuing disagreement.

The two issues that have most divided Protestants and Catholics in eucharistic theology over the years, as you may know, are the nature of Christ's presence and the relationship of the Eucharist to Christ's sacrifice. Of course, our dialogue took up these two themes. But in our report, these were not the first items discussed. First, we took up two issues on which Protestant and Catholic theologians in recent years have found some important common ground: the action of the Holy Spirit in the Eucharist (*epiclesis*) and what is meant by "remembering" (*anamnesis*). I will speak briefly about each of these themes, which not only demonstrate ecumenical unity but also suggest something about the eccentric nature of the unity of the church.

In the section on "*Epiclesis*—Action of the Holy Spirit," we were able to affirm the following together:[7]

> Reformed and Roman Catholic dialogue participants recognize significant convergence in our understanding of the action of the Holy Spirit in the Lord's Supper/Eucharist. Centrally, we agree that it is through the work of the Spirit that the sacrament becomes effective. While we agree that the Spirit's presence and work in the

---

7. "This Bread of Life: Report of the United States Reformed-Roman Catholic Dialogue on the Eucharist/Lord's Supper (November 2010)," 58–60, http://www.pcusa.org/resource/bread-life/.

sacrament is manifest, we also acknowledge that the Spirit's presence is inscrutable and the Spirit's work mysterious.

We agree that it is the Spirit who gathers and prepares the Church, as well as individual persons, for encounter in the sacrament with Christ, who has lived, died, risen, ascended, and now reigns as Lord of the Church.

We agree that in, with, and through Word and Sacrament, the Spirit makes Christ present here and now. Through Word and Eucharist/Lord's Supper, all that Christ has done for us, and all of Christ's benefits are offered and given. In faith, the Church receives the person and work of Christ. For both the Reformed and Roman Catholics, the Spirit makes present the whole paschal mystery—the incarnation, life, death, resurrection, and ascension. For Roman Catholics, however, a key emphasis of the Eucharist is on the one sacrifice of Christ that is offered to the Father, through the Spirit, by the Church in union with Christ. . . .

[The next paragraph is the one I especially want to highlight.]

We agree that the Holy Spirit effects and deepens our union and communion with Christ, the Son, and thus also, our union and communion with the Father and Holy Spirit. Through the sacrament, the Spirit also effects and deepens our union and communion with each other, and with all the saints who have died in faith. The Spirit forms us, the living and the dead, as the Body of Christ—many members joined together under the one rule of Christ, the Lord and Head of the Church.

The document goes on to note a remaining difference with regard to whether the Spirit unites the faithful with the sacrifice of Christ (Roman Catholics affirm that the church is joined to the one sacrifice of Christ and shares in Christ's own self-offering to the Father, while Reformed affirm that in the Supper the Spirit effects deeper union with Christ, but not as a joining in Christ's one sacrifice to the Father). But notice the significant agreement about the central role of the Spirit in the Eucharist. This has been a major advance in ecumenical understanding in recent decades, and it relates to our theme for today. It is the Holy Spirit who "effects and deepens" our union with Christ, and with the one whom Christ called "Father," and with one another. It is the Spirit then (not we ourselves by ourselves) who forms us into one church when we come to the table. Another clue to what it means for the church to be one: not by ourselves, but by the Spirit.

The second section of our ecumenical report addressed the theme of *anamnesis*, or remembering. What does it mean to "do this *in remembrance* of me" at the Eucharist? Many scholars have written about this in recent decades, and our dialogue shows the fruits of these efforts. The relevant sections are these:

> Together we agree that when we celebrate the Eucharist/Lord's Supper, we are remembering Christ's person and work in a way that goes beyond mere human recollection of a past event. In our liturgical practice and theological reflection, Roman Catholic and Reformed Christians share a common sense of *anamnesis* as a making present of and participation in the person, work, and benefits of Christ, through the Spirit. This shared conviction has three interrelated elements.
>
> First, we recognize that remembering is intimately related to the presence of Christ. As we remember Christ, we realize Christ's presence with us. Our conversations about Christ's presence in the Eucharist/Lord's Supper, therefore, should be held together with our common reflections on *anamnesis*.
>
> Second, we agree that remembering brings about a participation in Christ that encompasses past, present, and future. Through our remembering, we realize not only Christ's presence to us here and now, but our very fellowship in Christ. This common conviction should be kept together with the shared emphasis on the uniqueness of Christ's sacrifice in which we participate. As we remember, we enter into the "once and perpetual" sacrifice that Christ has offered on our behalf. Through this participation, we also "remember" and believe that our future is entirely bound up with what Christ has done and is doing now.
>
> Third, as was said in the discussion of *epiclesis* above, the Church's act of remembering is effective by the power of the Holy Spirit. It is an act of God working through the Church. Thus we acknowledge together that the Church's *anamnesis*, through which is realized our participation in Christ's person, work, and benefits, is ever a gift. God's action is always primary in this event.[8]

Why share this with you? Partly to celebrate that we are not still stuck in the old debates between Radbertus and Ratramnus or in the eucharistic controversies of the sixteenth century. There has been genuine progress toward mutual understanding and toward common affirmation of what is going on in the Lord's Supper. But even more than the fact of mutual understanding, notice where the emphasis lies: in the action of the Spirit, which enables our participation in Christ and our communion with each

8. Ibid., 60–61.

other. Hear the common affirmation that "God's action is always primary in this event." And in its discussion of anamnesis, the document also focuses on our union *in Christ*—this too is critical to undercut any illusion that our unity will be easily or obviously achieved through our actions. It is in Christ that we are one. Our remembering is not about our accomplished intellectual act but our dynamic participation in the one who acts on our behalf. As it says, "our future is entirely bound up with what Christ has done and is doing now."

What might all of this show us about the unity of the church? It is the Spirit's work, not ours. And it is about our unity in Christ, who has gone before us (both past and future) At the table, through our celebrations, we pray that the Spirit may be at work binding us to Christ and to one another. But it is not a work we can accomplish. "By your Spirit make us one with Christ," we pray, "that we may be one with all who share this feast, united in ministry in every place."[9]

3. How Might We Better Embody the Church's Unity in Our Celebrations?

Here let me just gather up the crumbs I have already scattered along the way:

- Celebrate the Eucharist as a meal that nourishes our common humanity. By focusing on the bread and cup as actual bread and actual drink, accompanied by stories of Jesus' own meals and recoghition of real hunger in the world, we better embody our dependence on God's providential care for our very being.

- Acknowledge at the table that we are all sinners dependent on God's grace. By recognizing how the risen Jesus confronts us all with our betrayals, and yet forgives us and calls us anyway, we disclose our common need for forgiveness.

- Do not hide the divisions in the Christian family, nor make an idol of our common understanding. Concretely, you might look for ways to acknowledge that Christians do not all agree on what exactly is happening in the Eucharist, and that there is ongoing argument (much of it more fruitful and civil now than it used to be) about how Christ is

9. "Great Thanksgiving A," in Presbyterian Church (USA), Theology and Worship Ministry Unit, *Book of Common Worship* (Louisville: Westminster John Knox, 1993) 72.

present, who is invited, and who decides. Yet in the midst of all that difference, we can rightly celebrate that the table stands as a witness to the triune holy One who lies beyond our understanding, who has come to us in Christ Jesus and continues to meet us by the power of the Spirit, in ways that remain mysterious.

- Seek opportunities to link genuine reconciliation to the celebration of the Supper. Perhaps you do not want to re-institute the consistory in the way it was practiced in Geneva, but people often need embodied practices that enable them to pray for healing and reconciliation and to approach each other with honesty to make steps in that direction.

- Focus attention on the central symbols of God's mercy rather than the question of boundaries. Proclaim the good news with vivid clarity. Invite the congregation to announce together the faith we share in the triune God. Celebrate the meal with symbols and gestures that speak clearly of the astonishing mercy of God.

- Attend to our eccentric oneness that is rooted in the triune God:

    - By the *epiclesis*/activity of the Holy Spirit—so the oneness of the meal depends not on us, but on God's living, active energy. Our unity depends not on our ability to manufacture it, but on the Spirit who binds us together. (so call on the Spirit, recognize that our unity is something for which we pray and long)

    - Because it lives from the memory/*anamnesis* of the one Christ, who suffered and died. The brokenness of the bread and the blood poured out has been variously interpreted, but is always at the core of the practice.

    - Rooted in faith in one God, who exceeds our multiplicity (which was the faith of Jesus)

We like to think of the Lord's Supper as a celebration of the church's unity. We proclaim that we who are many are one, because we partake of the one bread. But often this stands as an abstract and even false claim in the face of the bitter divides within Christianity when it comes to the table. In the midst of the divisions, how does the Eucharist testify to the church's unity? Only if we embrace our eccentricity, and recognize that the Supper proclaims faith not in itself, and not in our activity, but in the triune God.

6

The Eucharist and Communion with God

Francesca Aran Murphy

1. Self-Communication

HUMAN BEINGS ENJOY COMMUNICATING with others: they will transcend most material obstacles in order to send something of themselves to other persons. Lock a man in a prison cell and he will figure out a system of taps to commune with the guy slammed up next door. Lock a whole civilization of human beings in little pink houses and office cubicles and they will soon figure out a way to be tapping away, exposing their private lives via Facebook. Once our opportunities to gather in clubs and bars had diminished, we spontaneously overcame the resultant isolation through vulgar social networking. Jokes and funny photos make their way across the Internet like pollination in the park on a spring day. This urge to communicate is overpowering, in that it wells up and overflows into, for instance, the constant posting of YouTube music videos on which none of one's so-called friends ever clicks. One that is worth checking out is Eric Shelman's cover of "The Letter."

The human enjoyment of communication is likewise exhibited by our enjoyment of teaching, and of learning too. Arguing against the notion that altruism is no real part of our natures, the fine atheist philosopher David Stove observed that human pedagogical efforts extend much further than the educational projects of other species. Where nonhuman pedagogy of infant nonhumans is restricted to training in self-preservation, human beings will strive to communicate to their successors all kinds of things one could get by without. Perhaps both nonhuman animals and humans try to tell their successors everything they know. Stove claims that such human and nonhuman pedagogy is somewhat altruistic, or is at least a basis for altruistic behavior.[1]

If one could say that animals communicate involuntarily whereas humans do so freely, we could distinguish human and animal along the lines of volition. And certainly much human communication is gratuitous, or not delivered on a need-to-know basis. The problem with that line is that the human urge to communicate is overpowering. It's not an exercise of "free will" in a straightforward sense. It's more like a desire, and one that is overwhelming.

This desire is present in all animate beings. Animal and vegetable alike, all species strive to reproduce themselves, and in that sense creatively to "communicate" what they are. For all of us, human, nonhuman, and vegetable alike, self-communication begins below the level of conscious choice, even against the grain of conscious choice. When we observe the gulls returning to build their nests on the chimney tops, where, the year before, they lost a fledgling who fell to his death from the overly narrow plateau that his parents unwisely selected, it is difficult to claim that, on some level, these subhuman species do not, like us, *want* to reproduce themselves—even if their efforts are at times foolish and unproductive.

A tigress will fight to the death to defend the offspring of her reproductive prowess, her cubs. But she does not quite know what death is. To put it another way: on an animal level, all self-reproduction goes towards achieving immortality, in one's offspring. And, so far as the species survives, all animal reproduction achieves the end of an earthly immortality. So the tigress is content to "live on" through her cubs: she does not know death, because she "knows" and can know only the immortality of the species, not the immortality of the individual.

That sounds anthropomorphic: one may argue that not only does the tigress not know death, she doesn't know she is cheating death by

---

1. David Stove, *Darwinian Fairytales: Selfish Genes, Errors of Heredity and Other Fables of Evolution* (New York: Encounter, 1995) 141–69.

communicating her life to her offspring. Most of us know and mock those ideologists who like to speak of inanimate materials such as genes "wanting" to reproduce and behaving selfishly and so on. But only a good atheist like David Stove can really mock with a clear conscience. Those of us who are Christians acknowledge that such anthropomorphism makes a certain sense, since nature, however unwittingly, operates as if a designing mind were at work within it. There is an analogy between sending a letter that expresses deep personal convictions and physically producing offspring. The analogy is the creativity of both actions, the way the creativity is tied to reproducing something of oneself in another. If there is an analogy between producing books and producing offspring, the writing of the letter or book is closer in kind to animal reproduction, since through it, the author may achieve a kind of nonpersonal or virtual immortality.

In our self-communication we human beings do everything that vegetables and animals do, with a higher quality of self-donation. The next step in the argument seems to be to say that this self-donation consists in the fact that we do not achieve immortality through our children and we know we do not. We know that that bit of genetic material's continuation has no connection to our own personal survival and does nothing to diminish our mortality. It would seem that this is the source of the greater altruism in human self-communication: it gives rise to a person who is not me. And it would seem to be wrong that many parents do not reflect on this, and contrive to make their children into copies and extensions of themselves, seeking immortality through their offspring in a way not proper to the human animal. Perhaps, though, we should pause before taking this step in the argument. Is it really a bad or at least subhuman thing that the spirit of the parents lives on their children? It is untrue that "the good which men do is buried with them"—rather, it lives on in their children—and it's a good thing that it is untrue. The bearing of offspring was for a millennium the only image the old covenant had of immortality: is Abraham's desire for sons, and indeed God's promise superabundantly to fulfill that desire, and Abraham and Sarah's laughter and joy in the conception of Isaac *no image at all* of personal immortality? Not even a trending image, a pointer to the fulfillment of that desire?

What one is wanting to say when one distinguishes animal and human creativity along the lines of animals achieving all the immortality they can in their offspring and humans missing that goal is that the individual human cannot "say" everything about himself in his child, because his child really is a person in his own right, and so someone different and other. The whole of that fine thing which it is to be a seagull goes into the fledgling gull. The beauty of the tiger is repeated in little tigers so long as the species survives. That fine and beautiful thing which it is to be a human being in general goes into the little human communicated in the act of reproduction, but nothing of the good which is embodied in this personal individual. To put it another way, when we produce a child, we do not actually *create* the good which is this individual person. The child gets our looks, our genes, our spirit, but his individual personality, his soul, so Christians believe, is authored by God alone. We can give bodily life to another, but existing as a person is not communicable by human beings. The act of reproduction perhaps transmits the person, but it does not communicate or create it. This idea that the child in truth belongs to, or is authored by, God is brought out in all the Old Testament stories about God's granting a child to an elderly or barren woman, like Hannah or Sarah. Israel of the old covenant was forbidden from drinking the blood of animals, for the blood is the life, and life belongs to God: whether they know existence as a common property of the species, or as the personal property of the human being, that existence cannot be "secured" by us, because it is not ours to have and to hold. It's not a bad thing or a punishment that the "life," represented by the blood, belongs to God: it simply means that we cannot wholly communicate ourselves, because it's not ours to give. That is why the sentimental dream of replicating oneself in one's offspring doesn't work.

The word "altruism" does not quite capture what we mean by self-communication: for that we need the religious connotations of the word "sacrifice." In their procreative self-communication, and in laying down their lives for their offspring, subhuman animals are impelled by subrational love of their species, and this erotic drive obtains the continuation of the species. Sacrifice is always creative, because it is always a form of love. For subhuman animals, self-sacrificial "love" entails dying to "self" for the collective good of the species. The good of the species, the collective good, is higher than the good of the individual subhuman animal. For the human animal, the same law obtains—that sacrifice, as a form of love, is creative. But for human beings, self-sacrifice is not offered to the higher good of the collective, humanity, in such a way that the individual is extinguished, bowing before the greater good of the "whole." For human beings, rather, the act of loving self-sacrifice is an intensification of personality. The human being is at his or her most intensely "personal" in the act of self-sacrifice.

For humans, self-sacrifice even under the reign of sin and death exhibits both the absolute value of the individual person, and their deepest union with humankind. Herein lies the tragedy of sacrifice, under the law of death which reigns since the first sin: on the one hand, sacrifice as the highest expression of love for another defines our characters at the sharpest point of differentiation, but on the other hand, here, at our most personal, we are still subject to death.[2]

When we give ourselves for others, we are at one with them, and exhibit our common humanity, but we are also most fully ourselves, as separate persons. So the act of sacrifice is not an extrinsic "add-on," a result of "original death." Sacrifice is part of the way things are, with or without sin: the way things are, the universal law, is that self-communication both "gives the self away" and draws it to a higher level of selfhood. In our post-Edenic world, sacrifice is marred by "original death," but even in a fallen world it expresses the truth and reality of love.

The being of God, as Trinity of three consubstantial persons, could be called sacrificial, in the sense that God is tripersonal in and through acts of self-communication which generate personal "otherness" within a complete unity of being. The Son is Son by the Father's self-donation, the Father's giving of all that he is. The Son acknowledges the Father as Father in an act of attentive obedience which confirms, ontologically, the Source's paternity. Father and Son breathe the Spirit as the exhibition of their mutual, self-giving love. Each of the Three wills the precise differentiation and "character" of the Others.

We are always and inevitably at a great loss in speaking of God's dealings with humanity, for God's dealings with humanity effect a degree of altruism that we cannot comprehend, and call grace. God the blessed Trinity created the world in an act of wholly unnecessary, wholly altruistic self-communication. God the Father first loved us, and sent his Son into the world while we were yet sinners. And yet Saint Thomas is able rightly to say that it was "fitting" for God to become incarnate. It is "conveniens" or "comes together" for God to become incarnate, Thomas says, because "goodness implies self-communication."[3] He gets that out of Dionysius the Areopagite, but it seems a reasonably observable principle: jokes spread, seagulls reproduce, and flowers pollinate. It's "a reasonably observable

2. The point that self-sacrifice enriches the personality was made to me in conversation by several graduate students, whose names, alas, I did not write down.

3. Thomas Aquinas, *Summa Theologiae* III, q. 1, a. 1.

principle" in the sense that, if a Muslim friend were to ask one, "Isn't it insulting to God to think of him becoming incarnate as a man," one could cogently answer, "Isn't God good, and doesn't goodness want to disperse itself?" It makes sense to interpret our faith that God the Father sent his Son into the world to redeem it in the light of the principle that "goodness implies self-communication" and so "it is fitting for the highest good to communicate itself to the creature in the highest way possible," by incarnation. Divine self-communication is thus at the heart of our Christian faith.

Thomas goes on to ask whether this act of self-communication as "incarnation" was "necessary" for the restoration of the human race. In the strict sense, no, because the omnipotent God could have restored us otherwise. But in a loose sense, yes, because incarnation was the best way to go. It was the fittest way to achieve our restoration, according to Thomas, because it was the most self-communicative. Thomas gives six reasons why achieving it through incarnation best furthered the restoration of sinful humanity. Four of them are directly about communication and teaching: it built up our faith, to be taught by God himself; it provoked hope; it enkindled our love, "to be shown how much God loves us"; and it set us an actual living example to follow. A sixth reason is indirectly about communication: it delivered humanity from evil, meaning that it eliminated the bug that had broken the link between God and humanity. The penultimate or fifth reason Thomas gives is that incarnation works "as to the full sharing in divinity, which is true happiness and the purpose of human life. This comes to us through the humanity of Christ, for, in Augustine's phrase, *God was made man that man might become God*."[4] This reason sums up the other five: the purpose of communication is communion.

2. Sacrifice as Communication

In *Providentissimus Deus*, Leo XIII described the Christian Scriptures as a letter from God to humanity. In the epoch of the old covenant, the interchange between God and humanity was of two kinds. One was God's speaking to humanity and humanity's response, expressed in the interpretation and transcription of God's "Letter" over several millennia, in the long centuries between the exodus and the Deuteronomist. The second kind was sacrifice, with which the Mosaic covenant was instituted, and in which it perdured, over the centuries, even bridging the eclipse of the exile. The two

4. Thomas Aquinas, *Summa Theologiae*, III, q. 1, a. 2.

forms of divine-human interchange in the epoch of the old covenant are not easily separable, since God's word in the Torah has as it centerpiece the description of the sacrificial rites. Despite all the prophetic criticism of external sacrifice, no prophet exonerated Israel of the original divine command to sacrifice.

Did the Old Testament sacrifice express a genuine bonding and communion between God and his people Israel? Did the temple sacrifice express genuine communion between God and his people always, right from Moses, through David and the emergence of the state and its monarchy, down through the loss of Judah, the conquest and the Babylonian exile, the return, the rebuilding of the temple, Hellenistic conquest, Maccabean wars, temporary victory, Roman occupation and collaborationist high priests? Yes and no, and perhaps in the end a yes. There was communion between God and people in the act of sacrificing animals in the temple because, through thick and thin, both with a pure heart of praise and with unclean lips, the people offered this sacrifice as a response to divine command. *Nolens volens* they offered the sacrifice, and in this simple, maybe mindless obedience, the covenantal bonding between God and Israel held. A Jewish friend was once told by an Orthodox lady from Edinburgh that he must keep kashrut *because it is your duty*. The obedience of ancient Israel was not only thin, Kantian duty: obedience in sacrifice is a core biblical metaphor. Think of poor Saul, his kingship torn from him by Samuel, on God's command, because he did not sacrifice all of the animals and humans he captured to God. The contrasting exemplar is Abraham, and his desperate example seems to show that sacrifice represented communicating all of oneself to God, including the desire to be replicated in one's offspring and achieve at least an impersonal immortality. And so, from Abraham to Aaron, to Ezra and on through the Maccabees to the time of Caiaphas, sacrifice represented self-donation to God, and a voluntary, obediential return of the life that belongs solely to God.

Asking whether animal sacrifice really exhibited communion between God and Israel is like asking whether the covenant held good. One might offer a waivering no, a no that quavers in the face of the strictures of E. P. Sanders and the "New Perspective." We have been taught to see that like all the legal prescriptions of the written and oral Torah, sacrifice was not like Sisyphus' unending, unsuccessful attempt to roll a stone up an unending mountain. We have learned from Sanders and others that such prescriptions were not a Sisphyean attempt to *create* a bond with God, but were enacted within a covenant that was "always already" offered and sealed. It seems ungenerous to imagine that, in the late Second Temple period, "the flowing blood calmed the tormented uncertainty: are we still in the covenant."[5] Is it not at best an anachronism, a reading back of Christian anxieties, to imagine that any such "uncertainty" existed, say, in the time of Herod the Great? In fact, however, we know that at least among a tiny group of Jews, the Qumran covenanters, some such fears did exist: they were provoked into, as it were, sedevacantism, by confusion over the high-priestly line after the Maccabean wars. This group was perhaps unrepresentatively pedantic about who, precisely, was the apposite successor to Aaron. But it may be an excess of sociological thinking to imagine, with Sanders and his followers, that no Jew of that era accepted without perturbation the fact that prophecy had fallen silent, that Israel was wholly engaged in reinterpreting divine speech from ages past and no longer encountering a new word from her Lord. All the Bible's stories are about men and women receiving directly, or from angels, the word and the call of God. Did no Jew at the time of Philo wonder why such stories all describe the distant past? Was membership of the covenant intended to consist solely in sacrifice and not in a fresh word from God?

Moreover, this sacrifice was offered by mortal human beings to the everliving God. Though no doubt was felt that sacrifice expiated sin, a chasm still remained between mortal sacrificers and the living, eternal God. The fact that the Maccabean martyrs, with their self-sacrifice, loomed so important in Israelite thinking, and that the heroes of the Maccabean wars were believed to have been rewarded, beyond death, is an indication that Israelites felt that sacrifice could and should, in principle, bridge the gap between mortals and God, and create a true communion. But the temple sacrifice did not achieve that end: the animals' blood flowed, sin was expiated, and yet the sting of death, death incurred by sin, was not drawn. I am never wholly convinced by the claim that Paul first discovered he was fallen, and yearned for eternal life, when he met the resurrected Christ on the road to Damascus.

Nonetheless, one has to come back to the yes, to the old covenant sacrifice representing God's ownership of all life. The sacrifices of the old covenant bound Israel and God together, because in them is expressed the

5. Hans Urs von Balthasar, *The Glory of the Lord: A Theological Aesthetics*, vol. 6, *Theology: The Old Covenant*, trans. Brian McNeil and Erasmo Leiva-Merikakis (Edinburgh: T. & T. Clark, 1991) 389.

fact that life, really represented in the blood, belongs to God. Most especially, the first fruits, and the firstborn son, as standing most poignantly for new life and the hope of continuation of earthly life, must in obedience be returned into the hands of the God who has power over life and death. The divine "goodness" is exhibited in a terrifyingly "righteous" way at the exodus: the firstborn of the Egyptian oppressors are slain, while the firstborn of the Israelite oppressed are spared.[6] God's love is unsparing, and so the oppressed, too, are oppressing sinners. Who then shall be spared? Only when the innocent firstborn son takes the place of guilty humanity will sacrifice fully express the communion between God and humanity. For now the blood of the firstborn is offered to God in a sacrifice whose fruits humanity can share. The blood that is the life, God's creative gift to humanity, is made over to God, in an act of perfect self-giving worship, and by that act, made over to humanity to drink.

With typical astuteness, my friend and former colleague, Ian McFarland, once asked me, "So did Jesus cease to be a Jew when he said, 'this is my blood'?" He was referring to the Jewish prohibition on consuming blood: how could a Jew command the drinking of any blood, or say, literally and not metaphorically, "My blood is truly a drink" (John 6:55)? The prohibition expresses the fact that all taking of life is a transgression of God's ownership, an arrogant effort to seize what belongs only to God. The blood that Jesus selflessly makes over to God can be shared out, and drunk by human beings, because this blood alone is the effect not of the *taking* of life from God, to whom it belongs, but of the giving of life to God. And so the lifeblood is rendered back, and the communion Christ's sacrifice opens with the Father is opened between humanity and God.

God breaks his silence, with the incarnation of his Son. The Word becomes flesh and does so primarily in order to become sacrifice. In becoming sacrifice, it enters that space which, I have suggested, all our words and self-communication fruitlessly strive to overcome, the place of personal, individual death. In entering upon death, the Word of life becomes just a "thing," a corpse. The Word become "thing" is carried by the Spirit of love, the bond between Father and Son, through that empty place to resurrection. From now until the end of time, the church gathers around the place of sacrifice, the cross, to commune with the Father, through the Holy Spirit, in the sacrificial Son.

6. Hans Urs von Balthasar, *The Glory of the Lord: A Theological Aesthetics*, vol. 7, *Theology: The New Covenant*, trans. Brian McNeil (Edinburgh: T. & T. Clark, 1989) 395.

3. Self-Communication as Love

Every communication that we make takes shape in an effort to pass on something of ourselves to another, and to be acknowledged and received in and by another person. We can never say *everything*, not because we are finite, not because our lives are not our own, but because this exorbitant desire we have to show and to tell is broken-backed, always running through the distorting filter of our mortality. We never quite make a full communication of ourselves to another, because the force of self-giving that would enable it is not there. We cannot quite give ourselves away. There is so much left unsaid, even when our last words to one another are "I love you." The one communication that says *everything* and leaves nothing unsaid, no stone unturned, is Christ's self-offering to the Father on the cross. That communication of everything is accomplished, not by the divine person of Christ alone, but in the forceful love of the Holy Spirit. This communication says all there is to be said because, as actual, existing sacrifice, it embraces life and the grave, loneliness and communion. How lonely Christ is on the cross, as helpless as any and every death, watched by those who are helpless to save. This loneliness is an absolute act of communion with human beings, in their human condition. But this death of Christ is not offered to us, or made over to us in an act of communion with the human race. Christ's death is offered to the Father, as a sacrifice for our primordial sin, the sin that brought death into the world. This is evident in the liturgical offering of the Mass, in which we hear repeatedly that Christ's sacrifice is offered to the Father. The Father, who sent his only Son into the world, accepts this sacrifice and gives back the body and blood of the sacrifice to heal our wounded natures, indeed, as "the healing of our love."[7] Christ's self-communication to the Father, which says everything, exhibits God's

---

7. This is what Joseph Ratzinger takes over from Plato. Ratzinger writes, "Plato speaks of the reciprocal communion between the gods and men (ἡ περί θεούς καί ἀνθρώπους κοινωνία). According to him, communion with the gods also brings about community among men. He asserts that this communion is the ultimate aim . . . of all sacrifice and . . . cultic activity . . . he coins a wonderful phrase, which could . . . be taken as an intimation of the eucharistic mystery, when he says that the cult is concerned with nothing other than the preservation and the healing of love. . . . in the New Testament . . . the Church *is* communion—communion not only between human beings but, as a result of the death and Resurrection of Jesus, communion with Christ . . . and hence communion with the eternal, triune Love of God." Joseph Ratzinger, *Behold the Pierced One: An Approach to Spiritual Christology* (German ed. 1984; San Francisco: Ignatius, 1986) 86.

love for us and expresses that love in the shape of the Eucharist, which says and includes everything.

4. Sacrifice as Creative Love

The sacrifice of Christ is an act of creative love, the love that creates the church. The sacrifice of Christ is creative love, not only because it exhibits God's love for us, but because it reveals the nature and essence of the triune God, as love that is communicating, made over into another, and wholly united. The Father brings forth the perfect Image of himself in Christ, who is both other to the Father and yet wholly and simply one with the Father in the Holy Spirit. This perfect communion of the eternal Trinity is exhibited in the sacrifice of Christ, in which the Father sends forth his Son and, in the power of the Spirit, the Son is returned to the Father as a sacrifice of praise, as Eucharist.

The Eucharist, which makes the church, takes the shape of the sacrificial supper, in which believers commune with God by sharing in the life that is God. There the life that is God both eats with us and is eaten and drunk by us. And this act creates the church as communion. The question is . . .

5. Why Does the Offering Christ Makes to God Create Communion between God and Humanity?

We said both that obediential sacrifice to God is the central image of the old covenant and that the charism of Second Temple Judaism was perhaps marked by an element of "sheer" obedience, performing sacrifice not because it felt satisfying as a communion with God, but sheerly because it was known to be God's will. Christ's sacrificing himself to the Father engaged at the deepest possible level in the charism and spirit of the Israel into which Christ was born. His sacrificing himself was an act of sheer obedience to God's will. The Son does the Father's will not simply out of blind volition, but by the same rationale that makes goodness spread itself, that is, he does the Father's will out of love. And so, because he gives himself over exhaustively to doing the Father's will, Christ crucified and sacrificed is the perfect expression of God, the fullest incarnation of God on earth.

Obedience entails listening, and really hearing what the "authority" is saying, and communicating it for oneself, with one's compliant action. I mentioned Eric Shelman and his cover of the song "The Letter." Shelman started with a few covers on YouTube, and now he has his own page with more than two hundred covers of different songs and nearly four million hits. It's very good karaoke. What makes it outstanding is that he seems to listen to the songs, and imitates the singer so profoundly that he captures and communicates the precise emotion behind the original version. Jacques Maritain called the emotion behind modern poetry its "poetic sense." The problem with creative renditions, and every reinterpretation of "the divine Word" that departs from its poetic sense, is that they lack this obedience and transparency to the heart of God. So we can say that Christ, in his perfect obediential sacrifice, is the pure and "visible presence of God's acting and speaking in the world."[8] That shows how Christ crucified and sacrificed is the expression of the Father's loving will, perhaps, but it does not yet say how or why this sacrifice restores communion with God: simply seeing the expression of the love of God does not of itself restore the communion broken by original sin. One could say accurately that God's justice is rectified, and that God's wrath is appeased, and that the original "goodness" of the relationship between God and mankind is restored. One may also say that Christ's self-offering is burned up and "consumed" in the fire of God's love. As we know from Exodus 3, it is a fire that blazes up and burns without dissipating itself, the fire of the eternal "I am." For the eternal Son to be consumed in this flame would be to die and by the same token to live to eternal life, to be crucified and resurrected. Hans Urs von Balthasar states that "those who belong to the Son are to see him consumed by the love of the Father, which is possible only if they themselves are consumed by love of the Son." In this act of obedient self-offering, Christ expresses the very heart of the Father, and his own heart is broken apart (John 19:34), so that "my blood for the life of the world," the very life of God, is shared between God and humankind, like the blood of the Sinai covenant.[9]

Obedience expresses unity between one and another, and if the church were not the expression of the unity between Father and Son in this sacrificial offering, there would only be a "church" as a human institution, a human fellowship allied in human discipleship of Christ. The church is the expression of the unity between Father and Son in so far as the church is founded, out of the dynamism of Christ's sacrifice, by the Holy Spirit:

8. Balthasar, *Glory of the Lord*, 7:274

9. Ibid., 260 and 253.

for the Holy Spirit "himself *is* this unity of love" between Father and Son.[10] Founded out of the dynamism of Christ's sacrifice, that is, breathed forth at the moment of his death, the church is created by the bond of love between Father and Son, the Holy Spirit. It is this creative love that engenders communion between God and humankind.

6. Is Communion Two-Sided?

"Is communion two-sided?" is a provocative question to ask at an ecumenical conference on the Eucharist. At least according to von Balthasar, the real question between Protestants and Catholics concerning the eucharistic communion is not really the "real presence" of Christ in the Eucharist but whether we, the human participants at the eucharistic altar, ourselves *offer* a sacrifice to God. And we seem already, via von Balthasar, to have answered the question more or less on the Protestant side: in his words, "Jesus in his gesture of giving his flesh gives something that is itself in a state of 'having been handed over' . . . likewise, that the blood should be in a state of 'having been poured out' . . . Jesus . . . gives himself in the state of abandonment into the hand of the Father . . . gives himself into the hand of the Spirit who brings about the sacrament . . . and gives himself into the hand of the Church, who through the ages performs (*hoc facite*) . . .what Jesus' gesture of self-giving has placed in her hands."[11] It seems that all the giving and offering is performed by Christ and that we come to the sacrifice "with empty hands." We said that, when Christ poured out his flesh and blood on the cross, he acted alone, seemingly without collaborators or even accomplices after the fact. It seems, then, that in a radicalization of the Qumran intuition that the priesthood had gone astray, the Israelite sacrificial priesthood is terminated by the lonely sacrificial death of Christ. This is how most Protestants have interpreted Hebrews, with its accent on the finality and consummate character of Christ's sacrifice. It seems, then, that when we come to the eucharistic sacrifice of the church, our only participation in it is to eat, drink, and consume the self-sufficient sacrifice of Christ. It would seem that we approach the altar as consumers only, not as participants. It would also seem—by the by—that the Catholic stress on "active participation" in the Mass, from Pius X to *Sacrosanctum Concilium*, is indeed Pelagian, as some Catholics today say. It is a consistent theme in

10. Ibid., 255.
11. Ibid., 148–49.

the objections to the *Novus Ordo* created after Vatican II that the language of this new, fabricated liturgy is Pelagian. Before we turn, gratefully, to the language of the ancient Roman Rite, and to a liturgy Gregory the Great could recognize, one must observe that even if we do approach the sacrifice purely as passive consumers of the finished sacrifice, nonetheless, if God's sole command and wish be that we eat his body and drink his blood, that wish already diminishes the "self-sufficiency" of the sacrifice. You cannot say, "God first loved us" without implying that in some sense God needs us. If God wants us to commune with him by eating his body and drinking his blood, he relies on and needs our lips and teeth and tongues to carry out this wish of his. Even a wholly consummated sacrifice as envisaged by some readings of Hebrews requires that there be human beings on earth to munch up the communion sacrifice. As von Balthasar puts it: if God desires to be consumed, the church must enact this "service" for him: "This makes the mouth that consumes him an essential part of the sacrifice of the Lord. He does not act in the Cenacle as a soloist before an auditorum that listens to him, as an actor on stage before onlookers in theater seats. He always acts in such a way that he draws those who belong to him into his act."[12]

7. The Offering We Make to God

Let's return then to the Roman Rite itself. To me, this question of whether the offering is two-sided, offered both by Christ to God and *also* by us to God, is a genuine puzzle. It appears each week when I hear the prayers at the Roman Rite, supplicating God the Father to receive the offering. It makes me wonder, why wouldn't he? The lines that make me think "why do we have to ask?" include, for instance, these lines from what is called the "Offertory": *Offerimus tibi, Domini, calicem salutaris, tuam deprecantes clementiam: ut in conspectu divinae majestatis tuae, pro nostra et totius mundi salute, cum adore suavitatis ascendat.* Or again in the Canon of the Mass: *Te igitur, clementissime pater, per Jesum Christum, Filium tuum, dominum nostrum, supplices rogamus ac petimus, uti accepta habeas et benedicas haec dona, haec munera, haec sancta sacrificia illibata, in primis, quae tibi offerimus pro Ecclesia tua sancta catholica. . . .* In short, the notion that "we" offer the eucharistic sacrifice to the Father is there in black and red in the

---

12. Hans Urs von Balthasar, *Explorations in Theology*, vol. 3, *Creator Spirit*, trans. Brian McNeil (San Francisco: Ignatius, 1993) 234.

Roman Rite. The offensive "offerimus" occurs at least seven times in this most ancient liturgy of the Mass.

If the "offerimus" belongs to the means by which the Eucharist restores communion with God, our offering must be interpreted and understood in a way that exhibits the fact that Christ acts in this sacrament. If the "offerimus" means that he does not act alone, nonetheless, it must not be made to mean that we also add something to his sacrifice, coming latterly on the scene to throw in our two cents' worth. Our obediential human collusion in the sacrifice must be woven into it from the beginning, from the crucifixion *sub Pontio Pilato*. It must be present in the first human witnesses to Christ's sacrifice in such a way that our only means of being present at the sacrifice is by witnessing it as they did.

When we communicate with others, and when we do so most altruistically, we make them willing accomplices in our project of dispersing the goodness and joy of our lives, and making it live on in others. This is part and parcel of the fact that to love another is to will his good. It is nearly impossible for us to conceive that to will the good of another could be to will his death. And yet this is what Christ asked of his disciples, in the last weeks of his life: that they at least consent to his death, his self-offering. We know how Peter insisted, "God forbid, Lord, this must never happen to you" (Matt 16:21–23). We know how Peter resisted Jesus' intention to wash his feet. And we know that Jesus rebuked these resistances and required of Peter that he consent in his suffering and death. The women followers put on a better show. In Luke's Gospel, Mary of Bethany anoints his feet with precious oil; Maritain alludes to her action as the archetype of the release of beauty into the liturgy.[13] By anointing his feet, Mary releases the smell of the precious oil into the house, casting the fragrance over Christ's coming death and as it were incensing the sacrifice, releasing him to die in majesty. Christ is calling on her to make the "sacrifice" of letting him "withdraw to the Father" in "agreement with the movement of the Resurrection itself, with his coming from the realm of the dead and his rising up to the heavenly realm, the single, solitary movement of Christ—but a movement that wishes to be accompanied by the agreement of those who love and have been redeemed: *personam Ecclesiae gerens*."[14] Peter and the Marys are not called to *want Christ to die instead of them*: more humanly, they *are* called

13. Jacques Maritain, *Art and Scholasticism, with Other Essays*, trans. J. F. Scanlan (London: Sheed & Ward, 1943) 81.

14. Balthasar, *Explorations*, 3:266.

to let him go to Calvary, and to his self-offering to the Father. This is what the church does when "offerimus," we offer his sacrifice: we consent in it, in an act of humble obedience like that of all the Old Testament heroes and heroines. The line of Old Testament heroes reaches its culmination of course in Mary, the Mother who stood silently at the foot of the cross. This silence was the most active participation in the sacrifice, for it entailed consent to the horrible dying of her Son.[15] The communion created by Christ's Eucharist reaches right into us and enjoins our consent to the sacrifice. As the examples of Peter and Mary show, God in his incarnate Word commandeers our acceptance of the sacrifice: God relies on us to co-operate with his original deed, not by doing anything in addition, since it says everything and nothing can be added, but by witnessing and participating in the sacrifice. The liturgical words of the Mass evoke the events of the one single sacrifice of the cross: as Matthew Levering puts it, "the reconciling power of Christ's sacrifice constitutes the Church ever anew not by repeating the sacrifice, but by drawing us into contact with it"[16]—and when we witness it with Peter, Mary of Bethany, Mary Magdalene, and above all Mary the Mother, we must say "fiat." One does not participate in a sacrifice if one watches it like a show. The words and prayers in which we beseech God to accept the sacrifice constitute us as accessories after the fact. We are not enjoined selfishly to rejoice in this death on our behalf, but to allow it to happen, by consenting participation in the sacrifice.

8. The Eucharist as Sacrificial Love

It is as if at the eucharistic liturgy the Father and the congregation hold hands across the altar on which Christ is present. For the church's attitude mirrors and images that of the Father. The Father has sent his only Son into the world to die, and must witness that death; the participating church must likewise renounce Christ unto his mysterious life-giving death. The Father and humankind are brought into relation, in agreeing to the sacrifice: hence we beg and beseech the Father to accept the sacrifice, and thereby to be once more in communion with us. We insist, in the words of the Canon, on the spotlessness of the offering, as a sign that this offering is the expression

15. Martin Mosebach, *The Heresy of Formlessness: The Roman Liturgy and Its Enemy*, trans. Graham Harrison (San Francisco: Ignatius, 2006) 131–32.

16. Matthew Levering, *Sacrifice and Community: Jewish Offering and Christian Eucharist* (Oxford: Blackwell, 2005) 87.

of our loving and obedient communion with God. Over this communion of the Father and the ecclesial body of Christ presides the Holy Spirit, the Spirit who powerfully turns the flesh of Christ into the resurrected, life-giving body of Christ, and the "Spirit of the powerlessnes of love" whose consent to Christ's sacrifice is "the testimony to the omnipotence of God at work."[17]

17. Balthasar, *Explorations*, 3:241–42.

7

Communion: A Pentecostal Perspective

Telford Work

W‍HAT WOULD YOU SEE at a Pentecostal Lord's Supper?

You would see a congregation in pews or chairs—perhaps passing brass platters and cupholders the way I did as a Presbyterian, or perhaps proceeding to the front of the sanctuary at their own family or individual initiative to dip a morsel of bread into a cup of grape juice. You would hear a worship band playing contemplative hymns—or perhaps slow, amplified stadium-rock worship songs, or perhaps celebratory gospel—with some of the congregation singing along. You would see quiet, reflective expressions on churchgoers' faces, and you might pick up the sounds of prayers muttered so quietly that you couldn't tell whether or not they were in tongues. You would probably hear the words of institution, though you might not. It might happen monthly or quarterly, though in a growing minority of churches it happens weekly. You would definitely not hear an elaborate or drawn-out eucharistic rite. And you would have five to ten minutes to take all this in before the service was quickly concluded and the congregation moved on to our *real* sacrament: *coffee*.

In other words, what you would see at a Pentecostal Lord's Supper would not be all that different from what you would see in a number of *non*-Pentecostal Protestant contexts. It may be the act that most directly resembles Pentecostalism's mother traditions.

The scene I am describing could be an Assemblies of God church in Chiang Mai, where I celebrated Easter in 2010, or a multicultural Assemblies congregation in Strasbourg, where I attended along with members of the Lutheran World Federation in 2006, or Christian Assembly Foursquare Church in Los Angeles, which our family attended while we lived in town, or Reality Church in Santa Barbara, a ten-year-old "nondenominational" megachurch in Santa Barbara in the so-called third-wave tradition of Calvary Chapel. For that matter, it could be any number of evangelical churches my students call "nondenominational"—either because they really are, or because few who attend know about their affiliation—and which may or may not be Pentecostal or even charismatic.

This is supposed to warrant a *Pentecostal* perspective on communion?

Definitely. Liturgical elements are always connected to one another. The distinctive elements of Pentecostal worship come together into a distinctive whole, so even an element borrowed wholesale from another tradition takes on different resonances in the new one. The Lord's Supper bears somewhat different liturgical weight in Pentecostal contexts. So it's a good idea to describe those contexts in some detail.

Liturgical Context

Pentecostal liturgy is decidedly kinesthetic, and both socially and personally participatory. The Holy Spirit's empowering encourages widened congregational participation. The tone of worship is joyful, expressive, often informal, and sometimes casual. If mainline churches remind me of my school's celebratory but sober baccalaureate service, Pentecostal churches remind me of graduation day, with just as much structure but more smiles, cheers, and projectiles. While Pentecostals and charismatics have a reputation for disorder, and while sometimes it is well deserved, there is much more order than may meet the visitor's eye. Church authorities typically exercise strong and even authoritarian pastoral and liturgical leadership to maintain communal order while encouraging congregational participation.

Even in services where biblical practice is less explicit—for instance, where preaching is topical rather than expository—the Bible is formally and materially central in the service, as the living voice of God and the congregation's canonical authority.[1] Congregational attention focuses on a

1. Geoffrey Wainwright, "The One Hope of Your Calling? The Ecumenical and Pentecostal Movements after a Century," *Pneuma* 25 (2003) 7–28: "The Pentecostals then

central lectern or pulpit, with the communion table in front or to one side, backed by a choir or praise band. The table may be removed during weeks without the Lord's Supper.

The liturgical consummation of a service is often a call to commitment or recommitment, often delivered as the conclusion of the sermon. This serves the goals of personal and congregational repentance and revival. Pentecostals adapt the classical evangelical "altar call" as a time for people to sit prayerfully or come forward, not just for salvation, but for baptism in the Holy Spirit, deliverance and liberation, healing, or intercessory prayer. Some Pentecostals practice footwashing as a sign of humble recommitment to all others and regard footwashing as an ordinance alongside water baptism and the Lord's Supper.[2] Communion is folded into this time for recommitment. An "open table" that invites all who follow Jesus Christ to participate is typical.

In the Catholic Mass, the clearest moment of recommitment is the saying of the creed shortly before the eucharistic liturgy, with prayers in between. There is an implied causality of the Mass's formal sequence: the Service of the Word sets the stage for congregational commitment, then intercessory prayer and Lord's Prayer, and finally Eucharist as a kind of responsive divine gift that consummates the liturgical exchange. Pentecostals fuse those elements into the one rite, with prayers and confessions typically sung as the elements are distributed. This weakens or even overturns that implied causality. We *might* hear and confess, renewing our baptismal vows, and only then receive what we ask for, as the Mass suggests. But we might *first* be offered "the blood" and only *then* come to accept its claim on our lives, gaining a new intimacy expressed in prayerful and even mystical communion. Or we might pray and rehearse Christ's story in songs, being brought into deeper remembrance as we eat and drink and arriving

---

describe their assembly thus (#96, p. 749): 'For Pentecostals, the central element of worship is the preaching of the word. As persons respond to the proclamation of the word, the Spirit gives them new birth, which is a pre-sacramental experience, thereby making them Christians and in this sense creating the church. Of secondary importance are participation in baptism and the Lord's supper, spontaneous exercise of the charismata, and the sharing of personal testimonies.'"

2. Footwashing is more prominent in Pentecostal denominations in the Wesleyan holiness tradition, such as the Church of God, than in finished-work holiness traditions, such as the Assemblies of God. Kenneth J. Archer, "Nourishment for Our Journey: The Pentecostal *Via Salutis* and Sacramental Ordinances," *Journal of Pentecostal Theology* 13 (2004) 79–96, here 84 n. 14.

at a commitment so profound that we are born again. The looser, plainer structure respects the messiness and variety of life.

Consistent Adaptability

Because Pentecostals know God is alive, active, and free—because "the Spirit blows where he wills"—we do not expect our relationship with God to be formulaic. It will be consistent rather than random, but it will not be predictable.

This helps explain why Pentecostals have well-defined liturgical forms and routinized services, yet are suspicious of so-called liturgical "ritualism." By ritualism Pentecostals usually mean loyalty to forms that are alien to the spirit of Pentecostal worship, seem to operate independently of personal faith, fail to support Pentecostal practices, resist creativity and experimentation, prove inflexible to adapting spontaneously during the worship event, promote congregational passivity, or domesticate the spiritual.

Suspicion is not just directed at other traditions' forms. My local Foursquare Church overhauled its own standard Sunday routine as leaders realized that it had grown forced and artificial. Thirty years ago it was a small, traditional Italian Pentecostal congregation. One day it dawned on them that visitors did not feel welcome with the tongues and interpretations and coats and ties. "Our time for speaking in tongues was awful," the pastor told me. (His father was pastor at the time.) "A long silence, then someone would stand up and deliver a prophecy, then another long awkward silence, then someone would interpret, usually with a Bible passage. . . . I could never bring my friends to church." The congregation committed itself to revolutionizing every aspect of their life together in order to become inclusive of their young and hospitable to strangers. Tongues were relegated to other events in the church week and to private devotion. The pastor went out and found a new worship leader: a graduate of a Pentecostal Bible college and the Guitar Institute of Los Angeles who was playing at a coffeehouse at the time. His name is Tommy Walker. Soon the songs were fresher, the coats and ties were few and far between, and the church was growing.

Every week among the throngs of people of every ethnicity and age, you can still spot the small core of white-haired Italians who made it all happen. They come dressed to the nines and sit in their usual places. One day after the service I went over to one elderly gentleman and introduced myself. "You don't know me, but I just want to thank you for the way you sacrificed to make someone like me feel welcome here," I said. "I hope that when my time comes, I will do it too." He looked at me as if I were from another planet. "Son, my parents were at Azusa Street," he said. "New things are what the Holy Spirit is always doing. We didn't change anything."

As you can see, I was still getting the hang of a tradition I wasn't born into. I still am.

Foursquare churches traditionally feature the words "Jesus Christ is the same yesterday, today, and forever" (Heb 13:8) in their sanctuaries. That exchange helped teach me why. *Liturgical adaptability in the service of mission consistency* characterizes Pentecostal perspectives and explains Pentecostal practices. The first Pentecostals interpreted God's breakthrough as the Holy Spirit's new eschatological availability across borders (cf. Acts 19:1–7). The Spirit had begun something new to renew, grow, and unite the global church. Following through has been Pentecostalism's consistent mission. The fundamental Pentecostal stress on "Christ the coming King" reflects the movement's apocalyptic outlook. This inevitably plays out in how the Lord's Supper is understood and practiced "until he comes."

Sacramentalist?

Early Pentecostals such as Aimee Semple McPherson called the Lord's Supper and water baptism sacraments as well as ordinances.[3] However, Pentecostals generally reject the formal category of sacrament. Most embrace a Zwinglian position on baptism and communion. Some even appeal to dichotomies between spirit and matter or divine and human. These are not grounded in strong metaphysical assumptions or Reformation-era doctrines of incarnation. They seem to have been borrowed from fundamentalists, who were the most accepting of Pentecostals in their first decades. That has not proven very helpful. Pentecostal theologians Wolfgang Vondey and Chris Green argue that "the way in which Pentecostals describe their 'ordinances' is at odds with the original eschatological emphasis of Pentecostal worship and life."[4]

3. See the section on baptism and the Lord's Supper in the "Declaration of Faith" section of Articles and Bylaws of the International Church of the Foursquare Gospel, 1977 edition, in Archer, "Nourishment for Our Journey," 84–85 n. 17.

4. Wolfgang Vondey and Chris W. Green, "Between This and That: Reality and Sacramentality in the Pentecostal Worldview," *Journal of Pentecostal Theology* 19 (2010) 243–64, here 260.

It is easy to see why a Karlstadt-style dichotomy of matter and spirit is alien: Pentecost and Spirit baptism are *all about* a new relationship between God and creation, "a decisive new change in the relationship between God and the world and thus also in relationship between human beings."[5] That change ought to overturn both materialism and spiritualism. Practically, that is exactly what it does. Thus, more and more Pentecostal and charismatic theologians speak of "a kind of quasi-sacramentalism, actively at work in people's lives,"[6] a "need to re-vision the traditional Pentecostal understanding of ordinances into 'sacramental' ordinances,"[7] and sacramentality as "not an optional but a necessary component for a fuller understanding of Pentecostalism."[8]

Where Pentecostals do embrace sacramental language, it is in the Reformed direction of a spiritual presence, with an emphasis on power rather than election. "Spiritual presence" does not appeal to them because of Calvin's Antiochian doctrine of incarnation, but because it resonates with their missiological framework and their personal and church experience. James F. White says that the real presence of Christ through the ministry of the Holy Spirit was a basic given of all Pentecostal worship.[9] Yet it takes shape at a distance from the Reformation's concerns and categories, in a way that reroutes pneumatologically around the old stalemates over Christ's eucharistic presence.

Those sixteenth-century positions do a poor job of articulating what is a legitimate concern among Pentecostals. When God complains that Israel's "hearts are far from me" (Isa 29:13 in Matt 15:8), he is speaking not of a metaphysical distance between flesh and spirit (as God does in Deuteronomy 4:12, "you saw no image"), but of a *spiritual* distance. It is expressed in outward misbehavior: idolatry, neglect of those who suffer, malice, disordered passions, and the like. It is not closed by some gnostic pilgrimage away from physicality, but by restoring grace in conversion, reception of the Holy Spirit, divine intimacy, and supernatural fruitfulness. When the Spirit fills a believer, the spiritual distance is overcome, without

5. Jean-Jacques Suurmond, *Word and Spirit at Play: Towards a Charismatic Theology* (Grand Rapids: Eerdmans, 1995) 201.

6. Veli-Matti Kärkkäinen, *An Introduction to Ecclesiology: Ecumenical, Historical, and Global Perspectives* (Downers Grove, IL: InterVarsity, 2002) 78.

7. Archer, "Nourishment for Our Journey," 83.

8. Vondey and Green, "Between This and That," 243–44.

9. James F. White, *The Sacraments in Protestant Practice and Faith* (Nashville: Abingdon, 1999) 83, cited in Archer, "Nourishment for Our Journey," 87.

undoing the metaphysical difference between God and humanity that is basic to our relationship.

The conviction that God works powerfully in physical events lends a sacramental sensibility to the tradition and to its rites of intercessory prayer, words of knowledge, signs and wonders, healing, exorcism, confession and conversion, baby dedication, communion, water baptism, Spirit baptism, prophesying and praying (in tongues or not), interpretation, ordination, footwashing, renewal, and marriage. All these are outward signs of that restoring grace. So the same evangelical students of mine who are disturbed by transubstantiation are just as disturbed by tongues and healing.

You may already sense that if Pentecostals really embraced sacramental categories, it would involve a distinctive and unusual appropriation of the term that might not be immediately helpful ecumenically.

Pentecostalism's liturgical trajectory runs back through America's black Church and Wesleyan Holiness movements, then through Methodism, and thus the Wesleys' Anglican roots and their Pietist and Catholic influences, and in turn the English Reformation's liturgical reformers Cranmer and Bucer. You can find all these influences across the movement. Pentecostals have been rather friendly toward received liturgical forms and the theologies that coincide with them—Lutheran in their stance on adiophora, so to speak. They did not undertake the thorough liturgical reconstructions of the radical and even the Swiss reformations. Nor did they immediately leave their churches or denominations; they only started new ones after being rejected by their own. Pentecostalism was not a reformation. It was a Wesleyan renewal, in which liturgical and other resources could be put to either conservative *or* innovative uses to refresh the faith. Liturgical adaptability in the service of mission consistency.

Yet it is not just another iteration of Wesleyan renewal. It was an eschatological revival—God's long-promised "latter rain" to heal the church and the world before the *parousia*. That means that something had been missing! The liturgical forms in and of themselves had not sufficed. In fact, God did not even *use* the forms of water baptism, communion, or foot washing for this new dispensation. Nor did God use any other inherited practice—for instance, the laying on of hands as in Acts 8 or the preached Word as in Acts 10. The Spirit just arrived on Christ's waiting ones, as in Acts 2. This necessarily relativizes even sacramental accounts of baptism and the Lord's Supper. Pentecostals could never be content with "the sacraments" in and of themselves, and they could never help but make trouble in sacramentalists' eyes. New developments have shifted their focus. In fact, Vondey and Green believe that spiritual gifts overshadow ordinances because sacramentalism's "purely symbolic interpretation of reality" over-looks the need for ongoing spiritual discernment of the Holy Spirit's par-ticular occasional actions. The Spirit's intrusions expose the inadequacy of those symbols in a kind of divine protest.[10]

You can see this altered perspective in the way prophesying and Spirit baptism have overshadowed water baptism and communion in Pentecostal experience, testimony, liturgy, and theological imagination. A Pentecostal theologian, Arlene Sanchez Walsh, claims that *they* are the primary means of initiation.[11] That claim shocks even me. Yet it rings true, not only in oth-ers' stories but in mine. All of life in the Spirit is potentially sacramental, in the sense that signs or instruments can convey God's gracious power. Au-gustine numbered something like thirty sacraments, including everything from the kiss of peace to the Lord's Prayer to Lenten ashes. Pentecostals could easily agree that the Lord's Supper is one of many such institutions.

Efficacy

This brings up the issue of sacramental efficacy. What is accomplished in the Lord's Supper? Here I begin with an observation from Reformed theo-logian Peter Leithart:

> The Supper is not only a means by which individual members are joined more closely to Christ, but also a means by which the Church manifests herself as One Body: We are One Body because we partake of One Loaf (1 Corinthians 10:17). Whenever the Supper is celebrated, the Church objectively and automatically manifests this unity—simply by virtue of performing the rite of the Supper. This ritual testimony to unity may be belied by the way members of the Church actually treat each other, but even here the Supper is not without its effect: it issues a rebuke and an invitation to repentance, which may, to the shame of the members, be ignored.[12]

10. Vondey and Green, "Between This and That," 263.

11. Patheos Library, "Rites and Ceremonies," http://www.patheos.com/Library/Pen-tecostal/Ritual-Worship-Devotion-Symbolism/Rites-and-Ceremonies.html.

12. Peter J. Leithart, "Sacramental Efficacy," *theologia*, http://www.hornes.org/theologia/peter-leithart/sacramental-efficacy.

The Lord's Supper "objectively" represents (in proclaiming Christ's death), applies (in assembling people at his table), and seals (in holding them accountable for their lives before, during and after). All of these have results, whether clear or ambiguous, visible or invisible.

But what about the *inward reality* of union with Christ? Pentecostal suspicion of the *term* sacrament derives from the worry that "formalistic" traditions "institutionalize" the Spirit.[13] However, what Pentecostals are rejecting is not means of grace *per se*, but a "mechanical use of the sacraments that no longer affords to the sacramental events a conscious encounter with the divine reality."[14] The Lord's Supper *can* become an empty formality, as Israel's temple rites could be empty formalities.[15] Our misconduct might even arguably jeopardize the ceremony. Paul's threat that "it is not the Lord's Supper that you eat" is a grave warning not to use the category of "promise" presumptuously.

However, consistent Pentecostals *neither categorically affirm nor deny* real spiritual effects. Not just for the usual reasons—because the necessary faith is invisible, or because the presider's authority or ecclesial order might be lacking. It is because God's acts are surely known only through *evidence* in and after the fact, rather than their *surrounding conditions*. The same people who insist on "necessary evidence" to affirm the reality of a person's Spirit baptism are going to insist on empirical evidence of conversion and spiritual maturity. And such evidence does not appear with the kind of regularity that would suggest that ordinances are either *sure* or *necessary* means of the kinds of grace they are usually held to mediate in other traditions.

That doesn't mean they *cannot* be such means.[16] Sometimes they are. So are prayers, healing ceremonies, exorcisms, prophesying, dreams, congregational singing, and the like. The growing popularity of weekly communion suggests that more Pentecostals are coming to appreciate its power.

13. Frank Macchia, "Tongues as a Sign: Towards a Sacramental Understanding of Tongues," *Pneuma* 15 (1993) 61–76, here 61.

14. Vondey and Green, "Between This and That," 260.

15. Even when Christ removes his lampstand from its place—that is, when a church dies—it may still go on meeting, even preaching and confessing and baptizing and eating and drinking and babbling, as if nothing had changed. And when Christ revives a dead church, the same practices will continue, now "not only with words but with power, with the Holy Spirit and deep conviction" (1 Thess 1:5).

16. Zwingli's actual successors came to a mutual understanding with Calvinists affirming Christ's spiritual presence in the 1549 Consensus Tigurinus.

There is a practical empiricism at the heart of Pentecostalism. Life with Christ is not formulaic. The way Catholics treat beatifications and miracles, but not baptism or communion, is how Pentecostals also treat baptism and communion.

In fact, the Pentecostal circles and practices that *do* treat miracles and spiritual gifts as received in formulaic or predictable ways are embarrassments to the broader tradition. While wise and experienced leaders honor biblical assurances of answered prayers and healings, they acknowledge that often healings do not come and prayers seem unfulfilled, and they cringe when they hear claims that "if you weren't healed or Spirit-baptized, you didn't have enough faith."[17] Seasoned, discerning Pentecostals know that a particular sign's efficacy on a particular occasion does not reduce to a function of our faith or election, to some abstract divine promise to act that is not warranted exegetically, some metaphysical certainty or impossibility, any other circumstantial factor, or even its mere "objective" form.

This kind of analysis is disconcerting to those who are looking for guarantees, especially as a bulwark against the absurdities and idolatries that pile up when people get desperate for God to act. However, our guarantee is *the Holy Spirit*, not some *means* of the Spirit. We have all the indicators we need: faith, hope, and love, gifts, fruit, and even just the confession that Jesus is Lord.

Ecumenical Promise?

So far my Pentecostal perspective seems mainly to have deflated rival perspectives, displaced Eucharist from its soteriological and liturgical center, and set up in its place this strange thing called "Spirit baptism" where it ought not to be. (Let the reader understand.) Along the way I have taken a Catholic stance on miracles that will upset cessationists and transubstantiationists alike, a Lutheran stance on adiophora that regards as adiophora something Luther, Trent, and practically all the rest have not, and used basically Zwinglian terms to describe an occasionalistic spiritual presence that yields effects that are often other than what most sacramental traditions claim. Is anyone *not* offended or disappointed yet? To the ecumenically minded, this surely looks not like a new point of departure for ecumenical

17. For a more representative treatment from a respected leader in the Assemblies of God, see http://agchurches.org/Sitefiles/Default/RSS/IValue/Resources/Divine%20Healing/Articles/Defining_DivineHealing.pdf.

reconciliation but like the kind of incoherent monster we have come to expect from evangelicals in southern California.

Bear with me, if you can. Pentecostalism may look to you like a loose cannon that threatens to set Faith and Order back fifty years. However, I increasingly see it as offering an alternative to that ecumenical approach, which has stalled at a level of accomplishment that is frustratingly incomplete.

Narrative Pentecostal Sacramentality

Pentecostal theologian Kenneth J. Archer thinks that when Pentecostals reduce ordinances to mere memorials,[18] they contradict their own keen sense of the transforming power of testimony.[19] Even evangelical Baptist Stan Grenz argued that the Holy Spirit makes ordinances more than mere memorials by using them to work in Christians' lives.[20] Similarly, Archer says that baptism, footwashing, and communion provide "a context for experiencing the redemptive and sanctifying presence of God in great power."[21] The Spirit's grace conforms us to Christ's image by sharing Jesus' reenacted story and thus the life of God.[22]

Is this glowing description how Pentecostals *do* experience ordinances, or how they *could* experience them? I doubt that the Lord's Supper would actually feature very often in many Pentecostals' stories of God's work in their lives. They tend to focus elsewhere.

Archer acknowledges with many others that work needs to be done incorporating ordinances more fully into Pentecostal life and vision.[23] It sure does. Over ten years ago I approached our pastor with a proposal to explore how to enrich our practice and appreciation of communion. What spurred it was a conversation with a churchgoer from a conservative evangelical

---

18. For instance, William W. Menzies and Stanley M. Horton, *Bible Doctrines: A Pentecostal Perspective* (Springfield, MO: Logion, 1993): "Biblical Christianity is not ritualistic or sacramental," associating if not confusing the two categories. The two ordinances, then, "are to be understood as occasions of memorial" (111).

19. Archer, "Nourishment for Our Journey," 79–96.

20. Stanley J. Grenz, *Theology for the Community of God* (Grand Rapids: Eerdmans, 2000) 514–18, cited in Archer, "Nourishment for Our Journey," 84.

21. Archer, "Nourishment for Our Journey," 85.

22. Ibid., 86.

23. Ibid., 81.

background who was feeling the pull of Eastern Orthodox liturgy. I didn't want people like him to feel like they had to leave us in order to join "the New Testament Church" that took communion more seriously. And I didn't want Catholics or Episcopalians who had been "born again" at our church to reject a powerful part of their earlier experience of Christianity in order to be "Full Gospel" Christians. So I encouraged the church to think more deliberately on how we might still practice communion in a way that was both natural to our ethos and style and more robust. My pastor's response stunned me: He said, "If I could, I'd do away with it." He is a wonderful pastor, leading an exceptionally healthy and thriving church, whose sermons I regularly learned from even while finishing a PhD in theology. He always took communion seriously in services; that was why his response shocked me so. In fact, one week when a special service was running long, he kept communion at the expense of taking the offering. But even after fifty years at that church, he had not seen much evidence of power in the Lord's Supper. His Zwinglian expectations probably had not encouraged him to.

Yet just this year at the same church, it was a different story. The church had never held a Good Friday service, but requests for one had piled up over the years. A number of attendees were going to services elsewhere, and staff were increasingly aware that going from Palm Sunday straight to Easter Sunday with nothing in-between left out some rather important details. So the worship team gathered together musicians, artists, actors, and thinkers to conceptualize a Good Friday liturgy. They polled the people going to other churches' Good Friday services, asking what meant most to them. One Fuller Seminary graduate presented his own research into Tenebrae and Good Friday services. These people considered how to make the service the church's own, rather than just using one from a liturgical playbook that would have felt artificial and forced. They shaped the liturgy over two months, reinventing it at least three times. They darkened the sanctuary space with nothing on stage but a cross and a lectern. The candle hearse (whose candles are extinguished with each reading from the passion narrative) rested on a table specially constructed for the occasion. It was set like a dinner table with place settings, and was built so that people would kneel at it.

At the reading of the Last Supper, the congregation was invited to enter the story by coming forward to take communion. Worshipers came and sat, to be with Jesus and his disciples at the table, to be a part of Christ's passion. The pastor had called a three-day church fast before Easter, so taking the Lord's Supper was an intentional breaking of that fast.

People came forward as they were ready and so moved. They used intinction, which was unprecedented at that church. At the table, people would pray or be silent for as long as they chose. So this part of the service took a long time: twenty-five minutes for 320 people.[24]

Response was overwhelmingly positive. The church will be having a Good Friday service again next year, as well as Ash Wednesday and special Advent observances.

That is a Pentecostal perspective on the Lord's Supper. One that takes it with imagination and seriousness. One that neatly folds in distinctively Pentecostal narrative, personal, ecclesial, and soteriological concerns. One that wasn't forced on a congregation but drawn from its longings, sensibilities, and creative gifts. And one that exploits its transformative power.

Disciplining Hospitality

I want to complement that doxological treatment with a theological one from Wolfgang Vondey.[25] He complains that "Pentecostals have not been able to work out a comprehensive ecclesiology apart from the sacramental and eucharistic categories suggested by the established ecclesial traditions."[26] This is a big reason that the Lord's Supper has gone undeveloped theologically: its ready categories come from outside and inevitably fail to capture the true place of the Lord's Supper in Pentecostal life and worship.

Vondey uses "eucharistic hospitality" as a starting point for a systematic Pentecostal ecclesiology that prominently features the discipline of spiritual discernment, which is both widely neglected in ecclesiology and dissociated from the eucharistic meal.

The practice of eucharistic hospitality, where Catholics share communion with Christians from estranged churches, is controversial, to put it mildly. The Vatican forcefully rejects it as a grave abuse except in times of "grave and pressing need," such as immediate mortal danger, and only among those who "demonstrate the Catholic faith in respect to

24. In light of Frank Senn's chapter, I wonder whether they were having a "symposium" with the Holy Spirit.

25. Wolfgang Vondey, "Pentecostal Ecclesiology and Eucharistic Hospitality: Toward a Systematic and Ecumenical Account of the Church," *Pneuma* 32 (2010) 41–55.

26. Ibid., 42.

these sacraments and are properly disposed."[27] Communion should only be shared after church-dividing issues and personal excommunications are resolved. However, a number of Catholic priests refuse to conform and offer the elements to ineligible Catholics or non-Catholics, and quite a few Catholics take communion among "separated brethren" (including some at my church). Pentecostals adopt a spectrum of attitudes from very strict eucharistic discipline to open eucharistic hospitality.

On this matter Vondey says,

> It seems that the churches would give a proper sign of their desire for unity and reconciliation by preferring the fasting of the eucharistic meal over a celebration of the sacrament in isolation from one another. Surprisingly, . . . in Corinth, the Apostle Paul suggests just the opposite: Unity is achieved by coming together and eating together, despite social, cultural, or doctrinal differences. The Christian ethic of hospitality is governed by a principal rule: "Examine yourselves, and only then eat of the bread and drink of the cup" (1 Cor 11:28). Paul discourages the neglect of the eucharistic meal and instead presents a universal rule of hospitality: Each person participating in the church's table fellowship should engage in self-examination and discernment before taking part in the celebration of the eucharistic meal.[28]

We might proof-text Vondey's argument thus: "Because there is one loaf, we, who are many, are one body, for we all share the one loaf" (1 Cor 10:17). It is not the other way around; we do not share the one loaf because we are one body. Vondey goes on:

> The roots for Paul's admonition are found in the Gospel accounts of the Last Supper, which confront us with the fundamental breakdown of Christ's followers and the identification of the betrayer. At the Last Supper, it is apparent that Jesus did not immediately identify Judas but instead involved all of the disciples in an act of self-examination. . . . Whereas only Judas is eventually identified as the betrayer, Jesus directed the task of discernment at the whole group of disciples to whom he can later say, "You will all fall away because of me this night" (Matt 26:31; see Mark 14:27). He emphasized that discernment is not only the task of those who may have come to the table in an unworthy manner, but of all who are

27. "Cardinal Kasper Backs 'Eucharistic Hospitality,'" *Catholic World News*, June 18, 2004, http://www.catholicculture.org/news/features/index.cfm?recnum=30301.

28. Vondey, "Pentecostal Ecclesiology and Eucharistic Hospitality," 43.

gathered together, the entire church. . . . The fear and struggle of
the disciples in their execution of this self-examination is vividly
portrayed in the question asked by each, "Surely not I, Lord?"
(Matt 26:22; see Mark 14:19). Moreover, Luke's Gospel shows that
the disciples moved from an examination of their own conscience
to the discernment of the whole community. "Then they began to
ask one another which one of them it could be who would do this"
(Luke 22:23).

Indeed, in Luke a dispute arises at the Lord's table over who is greatest
(22:24–30). It eerily foreshadows the situation at Corinth.

Long ago I attended a Lord's Supper at a young, small, independent
church plant. Our presider, a Pentecostal seminarian midway through his
program, innocently turned to Luke for the words of institution. He sailed
right into Jesus' warning that "the hand of him who is going to betray me
is with mine on the table" (Luke 22:21). Blushing, he cut himself off and
awkwardly picked up with the rite as he remembered it. But it was too late:
the whole room was startled at the unexpected turn in the passage.

We should not have been. The warning is there in 1 Corinthians too:
"The Lord Jesus, on the night *he was betrayed*" (1 Cor 11:23).[29] I do not
even hear that phrase anymore except as a flag for what comes next. But
it is in the tradition Paul received: Not *the night before he died*, not even
the night he was arrested or *tried*, but *the night he was betrayed*. And this is
where Paul starts quoting. It is as if he wants the saints in Corinth to recall
that the first to "partake unworthily" was Judas Iscariot, and the next eleven
were the status-hungry disciples who, Jesus announced, would also all fall
away.

To "discern the body" (11:29) is to "discern ourselves" (11:31) because, as Vondey says, "it is the image of the body of Christ that determines
Paul's imagination of the church. In other words, the bread and wine are
images of the body before they are images of the gathered community"[30]—a
betrayed and broken body, I might add.

This is not the communion *fenced off from* divisions that we usually practice, the communion *regardless of* divisions that naïve evangelicals

---

29. I cannot accept the translation of "betrayed" as "handed over," meaning handed
over by the Father. The other uses of *paradidomi* in the gospels suggest the usual translation. Also, if the formula were referring to the crucifixion, it would have read "on the
[Jewish] *day* he was handed over," which Paul would likely have had to reformulate in
order not to confuse a Gentile audience.

30. Vondey, "Pentecostal Ecclesiology and Eucharistic Hospitality," 45.

often practice, or the communion *in spite of* internal divisions that warring mainline denominations endure. It is communion *to heal* divisions. It relies profoundly on the Holy Spirit's gift of discernment, entrusted to whichever members the Spirit wills (12:11), to display at that one table both "the unity we have" and "the unity we seek"—because apart from that supernatural gift we will misperceive both.

> The ecumenical crisis at Corinth reveals that the absence of spiritual discernment is rooted in a failure to acknowledge one another as companions at the Lord's Meal. At the heart of this problem stands the neglect of the faithful to extend their companionship in hospitality to others. . . . The collapse of companionship at the Lord's Supper led to divisions in the whole church that were reinforced, in turn, by the divisions at the meal. The cause of this collapse is the absence of spiritual discernment, a deficiency that continues to exist in most theologies of the Eucharist and of the church in the twenty-first century.[31]

The Passover freed not only Moses, Joshua, and Caleb to worship God in the wilderness but also Korah, the faithless spies, and the golden bull's future idolaters. So Jesus' flesh and blood are for *all* his disciples, including his betrayer, and for all the Corinthians. "Discerning the body" means realizing the catholicity, the "for-us-all-ness," of Christ's body and blood *and* Spirit (12:7). This is why we are "answerable for the body and blood of the Lord" if we partake improperly. So the task of spiritual discernment is not to determine the *scope* of Christ's church body, or who is a genuine member, but to determine *what it means* that all who gather are members. That determination is to be made in our common life, because the Kingdom's heirs who eat at his table *are servants* of one another (Luke 22:26–30). In so serving we will no longer be divided, nor condemned along with the world (1 Cor 11:18, 32).

It is in this hospitality—at the table, at home, in the street, at the office, everywhere—that Paul knows the genuine among us will be recognized (11:19). The *corpus mixtum* of genuine and ingenuine[32] is the whole broken church that comes together at the Lord's one table. Some examine

---

31. Ibid., 46.

32. Vondey appeals to Augustine: "The image of the eucharistic meal as a threshing-floor complements the emphasis on spiritual discernment not as a means of skepticism, criticism, discrimination, or exclusion but of self-examination, purification, and care for each member of the whole community" (ibid., 51).

themselves and are freed to act accordingly—made genuine, even—while others are stricken and condemned (11:30–34).

Christ's unity is ours at the Lord's table, in all who assemble to eat of the one loaf and drink of the one cup. And it moves from there throughout the broken church's corporate life and mission—as it did on the first Easter when Jesus "was known to them in the breaking of the bread" (Luke 24:35).

Ecumenical Potential

Vondey's attention to communion's original contexts, our present ones, Christ's finished work, and the Spirit's illumination ties what the tradition calls communion's "objective" efficacy much more closely and persuasively to its "inward" efficacy. His proposal is characteristically Pentecostal in highlighting communion's focus on the marginal and the separated. The first Pentecostals were immediately aware that the Spirit's empowering ought to break down boundaries among ethnicities, the genders, social classes, and clergy and laity. They have been embarrassed when these boundaries have reappeared in their midst, and proud when churches display the more inclusive spirit of the early movement.

The ecumenical movement faces a similar situation. The church has been almost entirely unable to reverse the logic of schism, and our usual strategy of pursuing unity may explain our ecumenical standstill. Vondey's proposal suggests a similar solution. The Spirit's gifts, not our prior achievements, are the source of communion's fruitfulness. It may take the power of communion to restore our communion.

Readings like these might help us resist our long-standing habit of abstracting the Lord's Supper (and ourselves) from its biblical contexts and redeploying it in artificial soteriological ones—as channels of "infused grace," covenantal signs applying invisibly to the elect, mere memorials, and the like. They can also free the Lord's Supper from having to bear weight that it seems unable to bear.[33] (I am referring to eucharistic theologies that

33. Kilian McDonnell says, "All recognize that the sacraments, when properly celebrated, have great evangelizing power, that is of spreading the Lord's message and presence among believers. But professionals in the field of catechetics know that historically a burden was placed on the sacraments which they were not intended to bear. . . . Correct and intensive evangelization can lead to fervent reception of the sacraments, but correct and intensive administration of the sacraments does not lead by itself to a commitment of faith." Kilian McDonnell, *Charismatic Renewal and Ecumenism* (New York: Paulist, 1978) 13–14.

sound breathtakingly powerful, yet fail to respect the empirical realities in our churches.) Indeed, they may restore the Lord's Supper to a place in the constellation of Christian practices that is closer to the New Testament picture, where it is cherished and significant but does not tower over other practices as it soon did in the subapostolic period.

Communion's grace of intimate union with Christ[34] can be identified more specifically and helpfully here as the grace of hospitality, service, discernment, and restoration. A Zwinglian can still affirm the effectual grace of Christ's real presence—if not literally in the bread, necessarily, then nevertheless still in the body that partakes and discerns together *because* of the breaking of the bread (again, Luke 24:35). Christ is truly present *with* the bread in that respect, whether or not he is also present in the way Luther meant.

This grace is visible. It is the real presence of contentious neighbors around the bread they have gathered to share.[35] What Simon the Zealot, Levi the tax collector, Nathanael the recovering skeptic, Thomas the skeptic-to-be, Judas the turncoat, and all the rest receive is his good news that they are one in his sacrifice. The Holy Spirit searches them and quietly discloses that stark truth to their hearts. They find "the unity we seek" by honoring in faith "the unity we have." Communion's grace is in the way the Spirit's verdicts powerfully play out in their responses during "the liturgy after the liturgy," in failures as well as successes. Baptism and footwashing are similarly outward in their effects, manifesting the same relationships of servanthood. With apologies to Augustine, these ordinances are *outward signs of outward grace.*

This is genuine restoring grace. But it is not a cheap grace that gives us a shortcut whereby we avoid the hard effort involved in receiving it. Methodist philosopher Dallas Willard rightly complains about theological and liturgical schemes that attribute to the sacraments (or the Word) infusions (or imputations) of righteousness (or virtue) in which we remain passive beneficiaries of the Holy Spirit's gift of sanctification. These biblical passages describe cooperative grace. Hospitality is a sacrifice, after all. Here it is a eucharistic sacrifice. Faith, hope, and love are difficult. They are gifts rather than achievements, to be sure; there is no room for a theology of

34. *Catechism of the Catholic Church*, para. 1391.

35. Maybe they are rich and poor, but maybe they are just feuding or selfish. When one of my children takes the last ice cream bar, it does not indicate economic inequality, just a failure of discernment.

glory here.[36] We can only make this sacrifice because Christ our passover was sacrificed on our behalf (1 Cor 5). Yet the way of faith, hope, and love is the hard way of the cross, which is now our cross to suffer along with him.

Vondey's observation implies that the Spirit calls us not only to be hospitable to the ones who come to "our" tables, but to give and receive sacrificial hospitality at *all* the Lord's tables. That means I *belong* at "Catholic" tables, and even the tables of traditions at least as theologically confused as Corinth was. It is not right for me to stay in the pews at a Catholic Mass, or even to come forward and cross my arms. That amounts to fasting unworthily. Instead, I ought to come forward to receive—not to demand some "right," but in faithfulness to our Lord's command to do this in remembrance of him. (Ecumenically speaking, that is a truly unsettling notion. Which tables *are* off limits?)

Finally, such powerful hospitality forces Pentecostals and charismatics out of our too common smugness, insularity, preoccupation with "lower gifts," and triumphalism. Communion awakens us to the presence of the many brothers and sisters in our midst whose gifts and fruit are as powerful and genuinely spiritual as ours, if not more. And it condemns us for the powerlessness and fruitlessness of our eucharistic practice and theology.

Communion and the Charismatic Renewal

Are you thinking now that Pentecostal perspectives would set ecumenism back *a hundred* years? Vondey's eucharistic hospitality is not only diametrically opposed to the usual ecumenical approach but also a nonstarter among the authorities of the world's largest Christian traditions.[37]

Nevertheless, I am cautiously optimistic when I consider how communion has fared in the charismatic renewal, which introduced Pentecostal sensibilities into nearly every other Christian tradition. Charismatic liturgical patterns generally honor the basic framework of the sponsoring traditions. Which Pentecostal practices are appropriated, how they are

36. Contrast a typically Lutheran complaint about this line of thinking: "Pentecostals teach that the bread and the 'fruit of the vine' only symbolize Christ's body and blood, and is a memorial meal, prophecies [*sic*] Christ's second coming, and is commanded of all believers. Grape juice is typically used. Once again, God's work of grace and forgiveness is turned into our work of obedience" (Richard P. Bucher, "Pentecostalism," http://www.orlutheran.com/html/pentecostalism.html). I do not see how.

37. Though it presents intriguing suggestions for how to take up Marsha Moore-Keish's five suggestions; see section 3 of her essay in this volume.

redefined and appropriated, and what practices they displace are matters negotiated in each tradition.

Renewal brings faith, hope, and love to believers whose former lives were "cold" or "dead," strengthens zeal for evangelism, dampens formalism, and strengthens community roles for laity. This can cause confusion about the relevance of standard liturgical practices—consider, for instance, how a person's persistent convictions of continued judgment or guilt or sudden conviction of release through a word of knowledge could undermine the credibility of absolution or the assurance of pardon—and highlight the discrepancies I have already mentioned between God's supposed invisible work in the sacraments and its visible impact. Furthermore, "Spirit baptism" suggests a moment of transformation after conversion that has no sacramental sign or liturgical or clerical form in these traditions. All these can alter sacramental sensibilities from regarding sacraments as dependable highlights to regarding them as among many occasions for divine action.

As Spirit baptism comes through God's sovereign initiative irrespective of ordination, it can undermine rules that restrict liturgical roles to ordained clergy. (Why should I take communion from my personally heterodox bishop but not the Spirit-filled leader of my prayer group?) And because special retreats and meetings offer more opportunities for participation among laity accustomed to token participation or passivity on Sundays, some may see the congregational Sunday service as less spiritual.

However, for all the troublemaking Pentecostal sensibilities cause in these other traditions, the charismatic renewal has *not* caused an exodus from these traditions into independent or Zwinglian ones. Pressure is not building for thorough reformations of liturgies, polities, or even sacramental theologies. Traditions loyal to a universal, fixed liturgy have incorporated charismatic practices at least as well as churches with "free" liturgies.[38] The charismatic renewal continues to see itself as a Spirit-driven prophetic movement for renewing churches by restoring neglected gifts to their rightful places.

At least some of the time, that is just what happens. Here is one example. A powerful force for evangelism and restoration is the Alpha Course led by a succession of leaders at Holy Trinity Brompton. As of 2010, fifteen million people in at least 163 countries had taken the course, which has been offered in "Anglican, Presbyterian, Lutheran, Baptist, Methodist,

---

38. For instance, they may seamlessly incorporate prophesying or tongues in the litany's prayers of specific intercession.

Pentecostal, British New Church Movement," Covenant, Congregational, nondenominational, Roman Catholic, and Orthodox churches.[39] It is evangelical in tone, with a special weekend retreat on the Holy Spirit featuring a "third-wave" Pentecostal emphasis on Spirit baptism. When a course or a retreat like this transforms the personal faith of churchgoers, they typically become *more* loyal and more involved. There are exceptions, of course; but if Alpha were a factory for rogues and irritants and an exit ramp from local churches, it would not be so popular *in* those churches.

Communion and Charismatic Ecumenism

Charismatic renewal tends to introduce Christians to other believers in rival churches who have been similarly blessed. Their friendship further encourages cooperation and liturgical appropriation across traditions.

This has not always mollified ecumenists who regard charismatic convergence as a surrender to spiritualism and experientialism. Indeed, some worry about *oecumenisme sauvage*, a "wild ecumenism" that runs roughshod over the disciplines and rules that embody our orthopraxis and our orthodoxy. Our churches need to determine whether this growth in love is a healthy sign, a dangerous distraction from the rightful ecumenical agenda, or the further evidence anti-ecumenical loyalists were looking for that ecumenism is a betrayal of the gospel.

I will conclude with a suggestion of how we might discern the answer. The situation reminds me of the force that propelled Peter to Cornelius' house in Acts 10. Long after fugitive believers in Samaria had already crossed ethnic boundaries with the good news and *while they were already doing the same* in Phoenicia, Cyprus, and Cyrene, a special nudge specifically from the Holy Spirit (Acts 10:19) came to both Peter and Cornelius' servants. The Spirit set aside Israel's holy rules for conduct (not just regarding eating but regarding entering a Gentile household and associating with a Gentile family [10:28]) and pushed them into one another's life with the news that "God shows no partiality" and that "everyone who believes in him will have their sins forgiven through his name" (10:38, 43).

In Caesarea, the Holy Spirit was not willing to wait any longer for Peter to catch up to what was already happening elsewhere. "Kill and eat," he commanded, over Peter's protests. That dream was a sign that what Peter had taken to be division no longer was. Unity had not yet come; nevertheless,

---

39. "Alpha Course," http://en.wikipedia.org/wiki/Alpha_course.

God's own barrier to it had been taken away. People were to eat together who should not have, at tables not meant for that purpose, in order to learn that "there is peace with God through Jesus Christ," the "Lord of all," who ate and drank with his chosen witnesses. Means were now available to bring together those who fear God and do what is right (10:35).

That meeting involved evangelism at an ordinary table, eating once-restricted food (10:48). As the Spirit fell upon Cornelius' house without waiting for Peter to figure out on other grounds that he was eligible for baptism, so the Spirit has fallen on all our houses as a sign of God's impatience with our refusal to seek unity by practicing the unity we have. Could the Spirit be calling us to a similar scene of reconciliation at the Lord's hospitable table?

My school's campus pastor is Ben Patterson, an ordained and charismatic PCUSA minister. As a church pastor he had always respected the Book of Order regarding communion. Then he became chaplain of Hope College, affiliated with the Reformed Church in America. In that more confessionally diverse community he sensed a "yearning to come to the table together." Without dismissing the importance of table discipline, but for the "equally important" sake of "the larger meaning of the event," he began occasional communion services in the chapel. At Westmont College, an even more confessionally diverse school, he has continued the practice, tentatively at first by bringing pastors of our various local churches to do the administering, but now presiding himself with chapel staff and a variety of college officials assisting.

At Hope College the practice was roundly criticized by "devout brothers and sisters" whom he loves and respects, "who wanted to 'protect' the rite." Ben has also received pushback from a number of voices on our campus, including mine, though I have the highest respect for him.

He has never developed a sophisticated theological justification of the practice, but he has been unable to ignore his "visceral pastoral longing for us to come together." In these services he is careful to stress that some of our churches will not allow us to share. In that case, he asks that if a person's tradition guards or disciplines communion in that way, then he or she watch, and pray with those who partake. "Baptism and Lord's Supper are great signs of our unity," he announces, "so let's regard the Lord of communion and pray with and for those who are taking it, and pray for the unity of the church."

He sympathizes with critics' concerns and shares some of them himself. He even agrees with some of the issues critics have raised and respects those who would "fence the table."

"*Nevertheless,*" he says.

I asked him whether he saw a link between his relationship with the Holy Spirit and this eucharistic practice. "Absolutely," he told me. "There is no formal contradiction between our structures and forms and the life of the Spirit; but they are not the same." The complexity reminds him of the scene in Ezekiel 37 of the valley of dry bones: it is one thing to prophesy over the bones so that they come together. It is another thing for the Spirit to breathe life. "The life of the Spirit gives me some freedom to move in these [liturgical and ecclesial] frameworks." When there's tension, "I lean on the life of the Spirit. It is often messy and inexact. But life is messy."

Ben resonates with Vondey's eucharistic hospitality, saying it helps articulate what he means by "*nevertheless.*"

Is communion at Westmont "savage ecumenism"? The term seems too strong. Ben reminds me of both James *and* Peter in Acts 15. He appreciates all sides in the "no small disagreement" over the implications of Cornelius' conversion. He understands the arguments. He resonates with the concerns. *Nevertheless.* What seems good to the Holy Spirit needs to become good to us as well, not the other way around. This is not ecumenism gone wild. It is discipline of another kind.

My analogy leaves ecumenically minded theologians like myself feeling like I am right there in Jerusalem at that high-stakes, hastily convened, and sometimes heated gathering, scrambling to catch up with a happening that is beyond many of us. What a glorious mess. I am cautiously optimistic.

www.ingramcontent.com/pod-product-compliance
Lightning Source LLC
Chambersburg PA
CBHW020333100426
42812CB00029B/3110/J